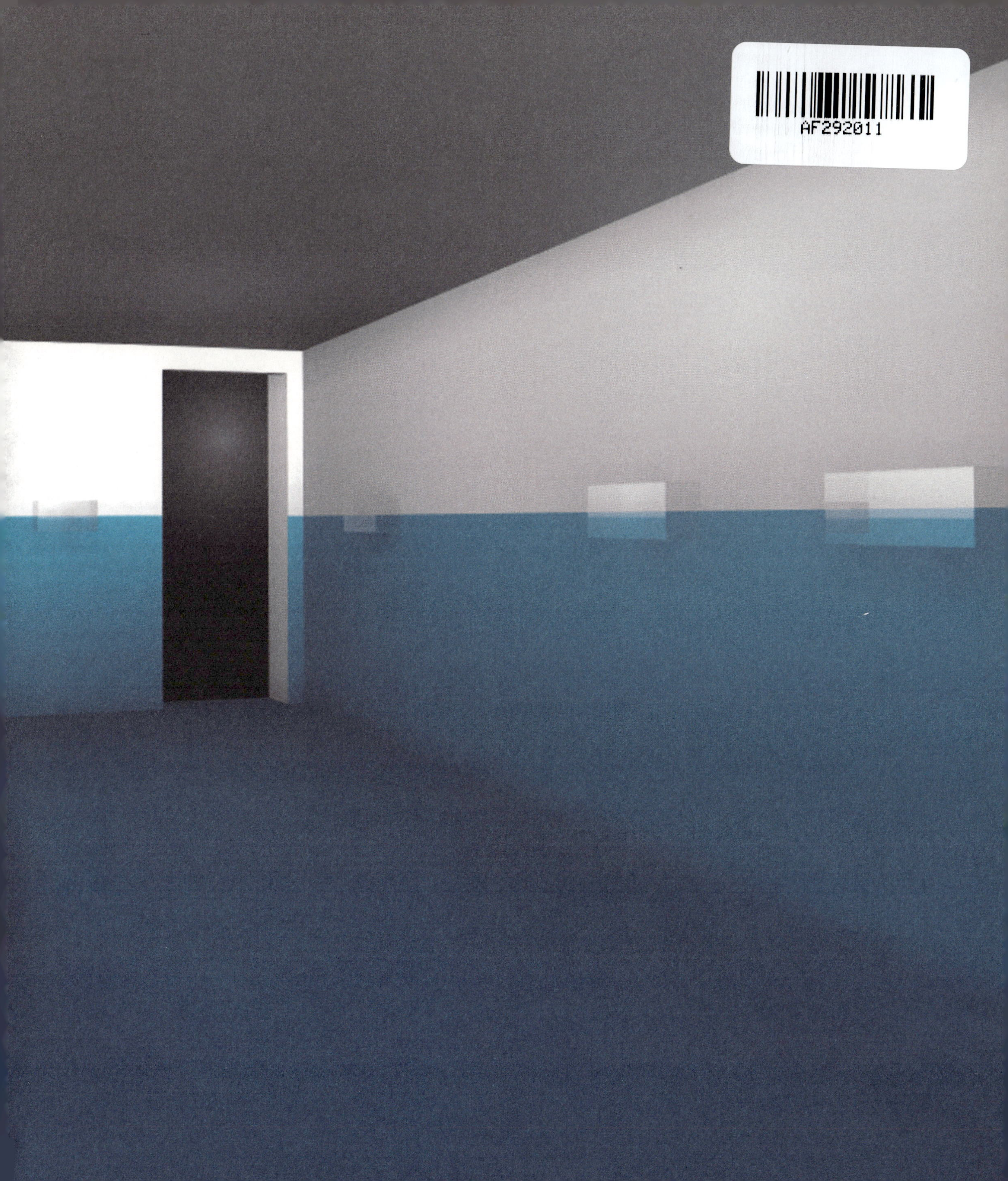
AF292011

Yuko Shiraishi

Temperature
Installation, Project and Painting

14 September - 15 October 2005

Annely Juda Fine Art

23 Dering Street (off New Bond Street)
London W1S 1AW
ajfa@annelyjudafineart.co.uk
www.annelyjudafineart.co.uk
Tel 020 7629 7578   Fax 020 7491 2139
Monday - Friday 10 - 6   Saturday 11 - 5

Latent Heat

A breathy purity I stalk
Of unheld colour, not grouted with dead stuff:

Colour as honesty, shakiness, seduction, sudden fate;
As irrevocable, steadied to humming greys.

Denise Riley, from 'Goethe on his Holidays.'

The first function of any writing about an artist is deictic: it is to point at the work. I apologize for using in my first sentence a rare word to talk about the act of pointing, derived from the Latin for the index finger, but it helps me feel bolder about making such an admission, obvious as it might be. This writing points towards the work of Yuko Shiraishi, which it considers good and affirmative: if not of life exactly then certainly of aliveness, and its offer of 'unheld colour, not grouted with dead stuff'. Her work does seem to combine the identifications of colour the lines by Denise Riley above make: colour as 'honesty' (something better than good intentions: acts of affirmation have to admit to impediments); colour as 'shakiness' (the fate of the necessarily embodied brushstroke); and 'seduction' (no gloss required). If we allow such drama, colour experience may be considered also as 'sudden fate' and as 'irrevocable'. Abstract paintings possessed of frontality are necessarily instantaneous, sudden, in their first address to the viewer.

    Certain types of work make one more aware than usual about what one says, and more wary. The disappointment that follows from a failed or partial verbalisation of anything that deeply matters is familiar enough. It is not just the writer's or the artist's concern, it is any viewer's also, and it may show in their hesitant shifting from foot to foot or a hesitation about filling painting's silence with words in its presence. Robin Purves: 'Writing is something that befalls painting, being provoked into existence by painting's silence, as a categorical catastrophe of surplus exegesis or as the unadorned and provisional recognition of "what works", which might yet allow yellow (say) to be nothing but itself and nothing it is not.' These difficulties are not based on superstitiousness. Nor does a wariness about speaking mean that the work is actually difficult. Good works of art – by van Gogh, Giovanni Anselmo or Blinky Palermo – need not be. Though I should not go too far in making this ease seem continuous with the rest of experience, from which it is somewhat separate. Art involves rule changes. Imagine breathing water instead of air:

> *Breathing water is easy*
> *If you put your mind to it.*
> *The little difficulty*
> *Of the first breath*
> *Is soon got over. You*
> *Will find everything right.*

Despite the insistence that the 'little difficulty' of breathing water can be overcome, this poem (W.S. Graham's 'Falling Into the Sea') retains, by virtue of not admitting to it, a slight disquiet at crossing the boundary from above to below water. It also evokes for me here a thematic insistence on a horizontal division in some of Yuko Shiraishi's recent work. This is of more than formal significance for the artist, and more than an echo of the architectural projects she has been working on to make actual swimming pools: it figures for her those boundaries between living and dying, sanity and insanity, which are understood as substantial and significant ones but also as traversable by anyone. The installation made for the back gallery at Annely Juda Fine Art, Anableps anableps/Cuatro ojos, consists of a horizon line that functions as a clear marker of imaginary water. Most viewers will find their eye level is positioned at or below the line which defines the blue of a fictional pool. Colour boxes, faced with glass, make an exhibition as though of surrogate paintings. The reassurances and affirmations of colour are disconcerted: colour here is presented as shifty, not quite available. And you are removed from the tactile aspects the paintings allow us to enjoy: opacity and transparency, the latent heat of a warm ground. As Richard Grayson has demonstrated, the dominant technologies of representation are apparent even in work such as Yuko Shiraishi's, whose paintings might at first be seen as antagonistic to anything abridged or lacking in immediacy. Simple as it is, the installation was visualised first with the aid of a computer. The realization of it as a space retains a slight digital chilliness, in addition to the temperature this particular blue entails. A particular inspiration for this work needs to be noted: a South American freshwater minnow called Anableps anableps (or more straightforwardly Cuatro ojos, 'four eyes'), which is one of the few creatures to have evolved an eye with a retina in two parts, that enables it to focus perfectly on prey both above and below the waterline using the same lens. Quite a feat, to see above and below in this particular way, but human vision based on straightforward binocularism isn't necessarily disadvantaged by comparison. According to Merleau-

Ponty, 'the inner horizon of an object cannot become an object without the surrounding objects becoming a horizon, and so vision is an act with two facets.' We may not have four eyes like the Anableps, but evolution lets us make good use of the two we have.

Shiraishi's move to exhibiting flatly painted installations as a co-presence alongside the studio work allows a strong dialectic to emerge. The paintings do affirm and compensate. A distinct shakiness of manufacture is evident, an admission that no colour will ever be applied with complete evenness, but this is the paintings' principle of honesty. They would never deny being made by the hand but do not want to advertise it too much, or sentimentalize what it involves. This approach also makes a satisfying contrast with what Barthes analyses, in his incomparable writings on Cy Twombly, as 'this fatality: my body will never be yours. From this fatality, in which a certain human affliction can be epitomized, there is only one means of escape: seduction: that my body (or its sensuous substitutes, art, writing) seduce, overwhelm, or disturb the other body.' Barthes has worked towards this point from the way we read the inimitable gesture and touch of Twombly's work back to a single body. There is surely something that is inimitable also in Yuko Shiraishi's paintings, but it does not advertise as Twombly's gesturalism does. There is certainly a seduction of the viewer. (I'm still not sure if its use of colour could qualify as 'sudden fate'. I'll leave that question to you.) But that which is inimitable in her painting is the way in which evenness of coverage of the surface, a certain tolerance of anonymity, is aspired to but not reached. Genuinely aspired to, all the same. This matters. Touch shows as something inevitable and pleasurable, but which is also required to operate under the limits of a modern discretion: it is perhaps only allowed to announce itself discreetly as a by-product of the task of building up areas of colour to the requisite density and opacity. As a work by Dan Flavin conveys to viewers that they too could go to a store and assemble exactly such a work from easily available components, paintings that show an aspiration to evenness of coverage play down the artist's facility and uniqueness. They do this in favour of an offer to the viewer of a form that can be appropriated: the feeling that you could do this too, or that the boundary that makes you in this case an observer rather than the producer of the work is not untraversable.

The democratic effect of minimalist art (and art such as Yuko Shiraishi's that acknowledge minimalism's compelling power) is still frequently made fun of but there was and remains something in it. Better perhaps to think about architecture for a moment to re-emphasize what is at stake here. Good modern architects remain suspicious of rhetoric (though they can be good at drama), and as they attempt to solve the problem of how best a building is to be used, many remain haunted by the idea of a styleless style. In practice of course it is never achieved, though the honesty with which it is not achieved is legible, whatever the decade, the budget, the informing ideas. The life a modern building acquires in use, and the pleasure it offers, is most convincing when given to people as their own idea. Most architecture is experienced inattentively, but well designed buildings allow us to appropriate them for pleasure in use without realizing that that is what we are quite naturally doing. You take the covered way by the field open to the air, a built equivalent of a line of shade trees, to enjoy the feeling of being outside and inside at the same time; you sit on the bench with its back to the spacious stairwell, you don't have to actually look in that direction, in fact not doing so allows you to feel surprised by the friend you have arranged to meet, and for whom you have arrived early. These are properly architectural questions. It is not possible here to look in detail at Yuko Shiraishi's work with architects, notably her superb collaboration with Allies and Morrison on the BBC Media Centre, but, even if briefly, it's important to note that her work shows a deep connection with the pursuit of the never to be achieved style-without-style that still informs good modern architecture.

Shiraishi's compositional procedures in her recent paintings involve a tolerance of systematic exploration (of the orders produced by varying widths and numbers of bands, for example) that is at the same time idiosyncratic, productive of individual works, but not, at first sight, wildly or demonstrably so. But to reiterate any idea of restraint is to risk making them seem more well balanced than they are. There is discretion but also drama here too, the drama by which unheld colour is enabled and disclosed. Narrow yellow bands find yellow in the pink-orange ground, orange when thinly painted, pinker when fat. A jade ground appears to admit no previous ground colour to show through; but the warm brick-pink lines find out the yellow in this seemingly absolute green. A stained magenta ground should not feel cold, but it does. And there are encounters that paintings hold out as possible but which never quite happen. In *Blink 2*, a warm green is overlaid by bands of lilac. The variation in ground colour means these bands are sometimes lighter, sometimes darker than the green, but because the lilac bands are themselves edged top and bottom by lilac of a paler hue, you never get a chance to make that comparison of weight fairly and squarely. You can see it from a distance, know that the two colours are teetering in a fine balance, but on this occasion can apply no detective's truth-test by close examination. The surface is more eventful than many of the other paintings, but paradoxically you are sent away from it, back to the long view, to grasp the balance that is at stake in the painting. It's important also that sometimes the pencil and crayon lines show, and that the means by which edges retain colour in an identifiable area are manual, not mechanical. The edges remain straight but the density of the paint either side can never quite find uniformity, to which it does not entirely aspire. The optical shimmer interacts with this variety of pressure so that the near view cannot be reconciled with the view from further off, as the interior of a Judd box can't be put together again with its exterior. But the resources of the painting, here an insistence on multiple horizons, mean that the slightest tilt of the head releases the ground colour from its status as 'ground', which cannot be thought its definitive identity.

These are paintings for daylight; or for the times of day, evening and morning, when local colour is allowed more to show as what it actually is by the prevailing pull of those hours to the bluer end of the spectrum. Though even as such times hold out the promise of knowing and fixing colour 'as it actually is', you know the absurdity of that thought too, that any colour could be definitively secured and identified. And there is no need for that to be a grand or exalted dilemma either, it can be as ordinary and affirmative as water; or as any day can be, when you allow it or when it is allowed. In 'L'Heure Bleue' by Edward Gorey, the first illustration shows two creatures, our heroes, seated in tall armchairs by the French windows. Their room, with its over-active wallpaper and carpet, opens on to a balcony and the insistent blue of evening. (Goethe: 'But as we readily follow an agreeable object that flies from us, so we love to contemplate blue, not because it advances to us, but because it draws us after it.'). What one creature says to the other is first a thought that aspires to be as profound as blue, and second a sentence, perfect in its punctuation, that bumps back to earth: 'It is not the living, it is the being lived on. / I must remember to write that, along with some other things, down.' They can't find the words for blue, but that's all right.

Ian Hunt, July 2005

References:

Denise Riley, 'Goethe on his Holidays' from Selected Poems, Reality Street Editions, 2000
Robin Purves, 'Denise Riley passim', The Gig 9, Willowdale, Ontario, September 2001
W.S. Graham, 'Falling into the Sea' from New Collected Poems ed. Matthew Francis, Faber 2004
Richard Grayson, 'Making Space', Tuesday is Cerise, Northumbria University Fine Art Press, 2005
Maurice Merleau-Ponty, 'Phenomenology of Perception' [1945], tr. Colin Smith, Routledge, 2003, p.78
Roland Barthes, 'Cy Twombly: Works on Paper', The Responsibility of Forms, tr. Richard Howard, University of California, 1991
Goethe from 'Art in Theory 1648-1815', eds. Harrison Wood, Gaiger, Blackwell
Edward Gorey, 'L'Heure Bleue', Amphigorey Also, Harcourt Brace Jovanovich, 1983

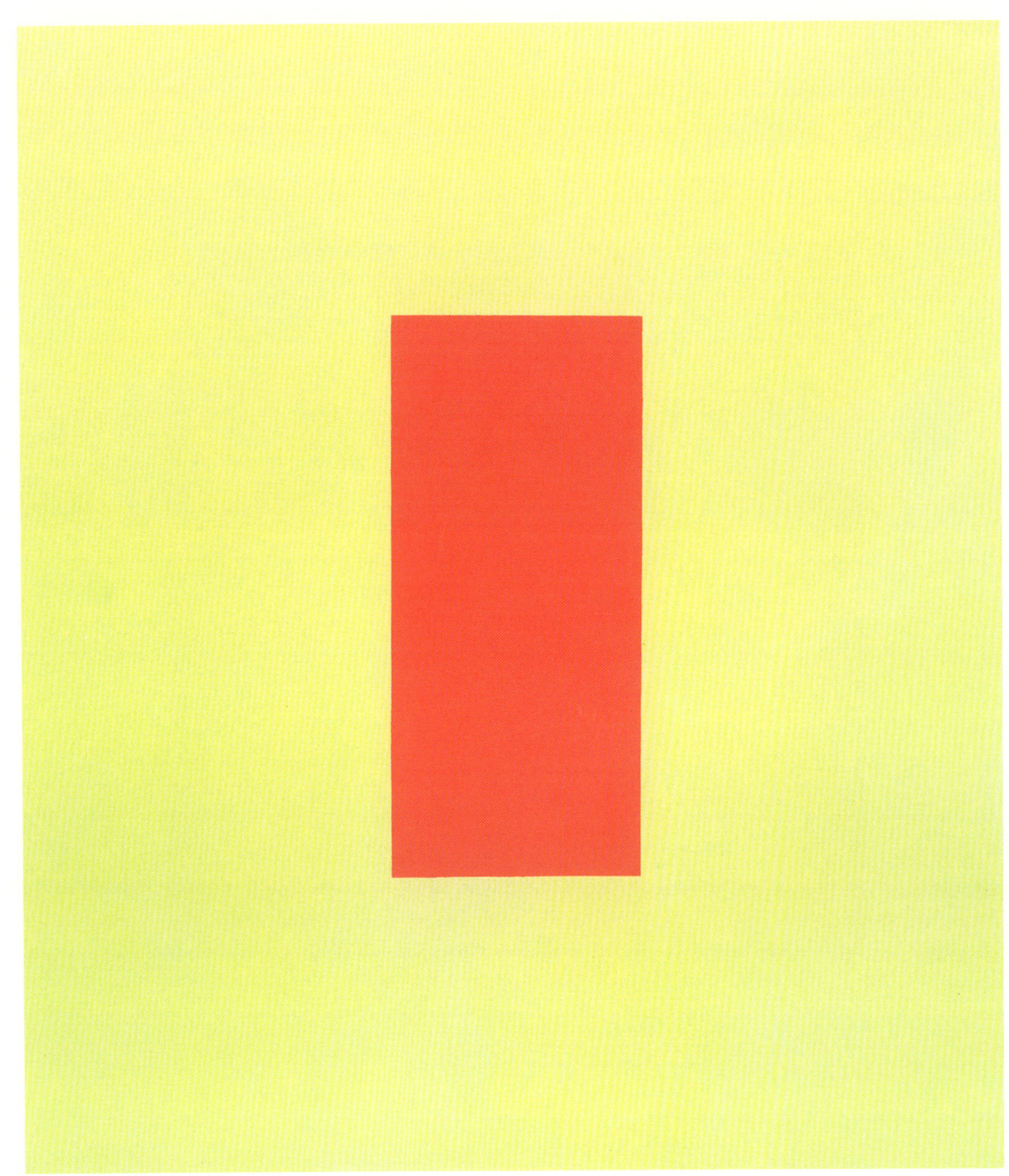

Entrance   2005
oil on canvas 137 x 122 cm

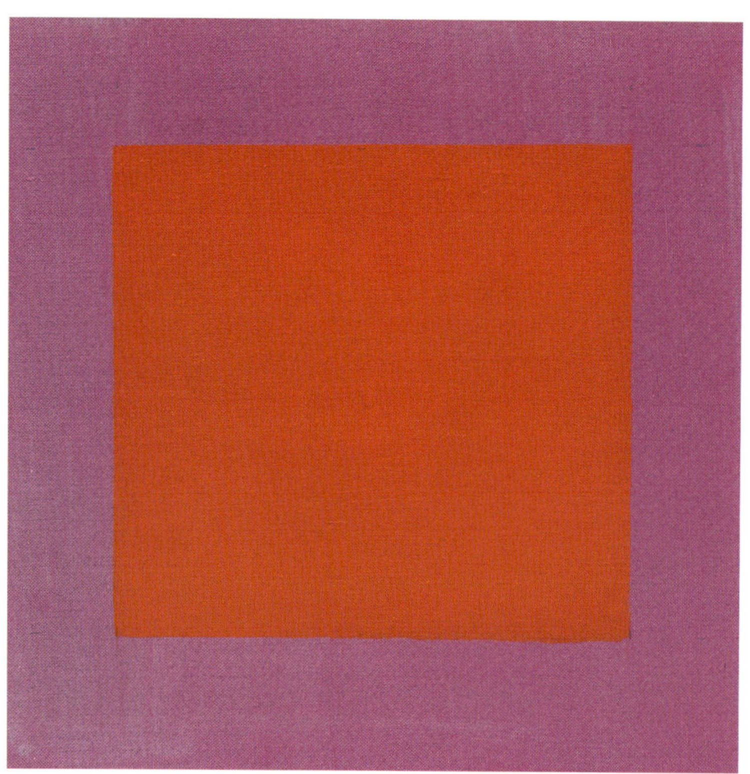

Vermilion Square   2005
oil on canvas 33 x 33 cm

Flux (5)   2004
oil on canvas 167.8 x 152 cm

Forest (3)   2004
oil on canvas 137 x 122 cm

Flux (8)   2004
oil on canvas 152 x 137 cm

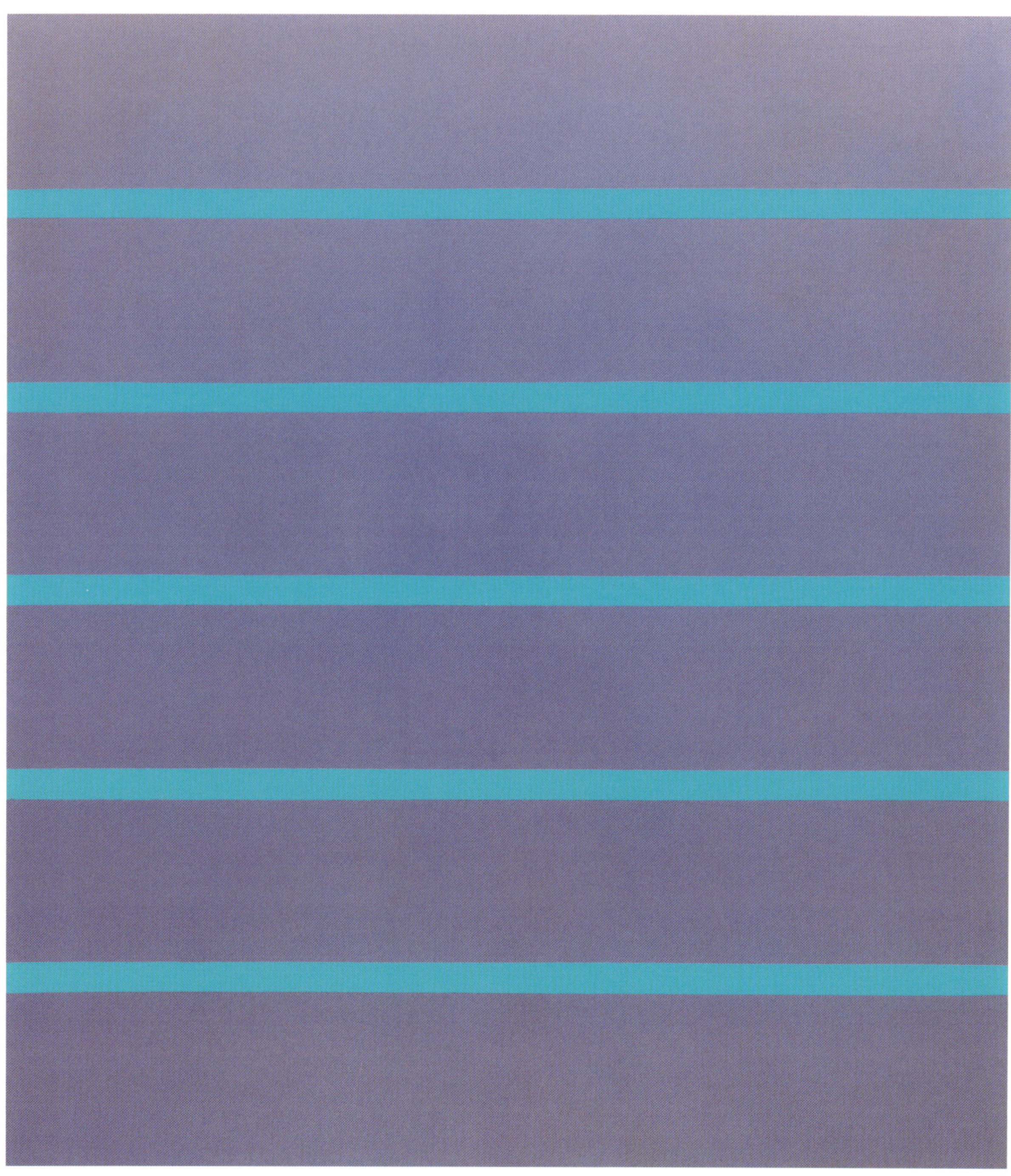

Light Night   2005
oil on canvas   152 x 137 cm

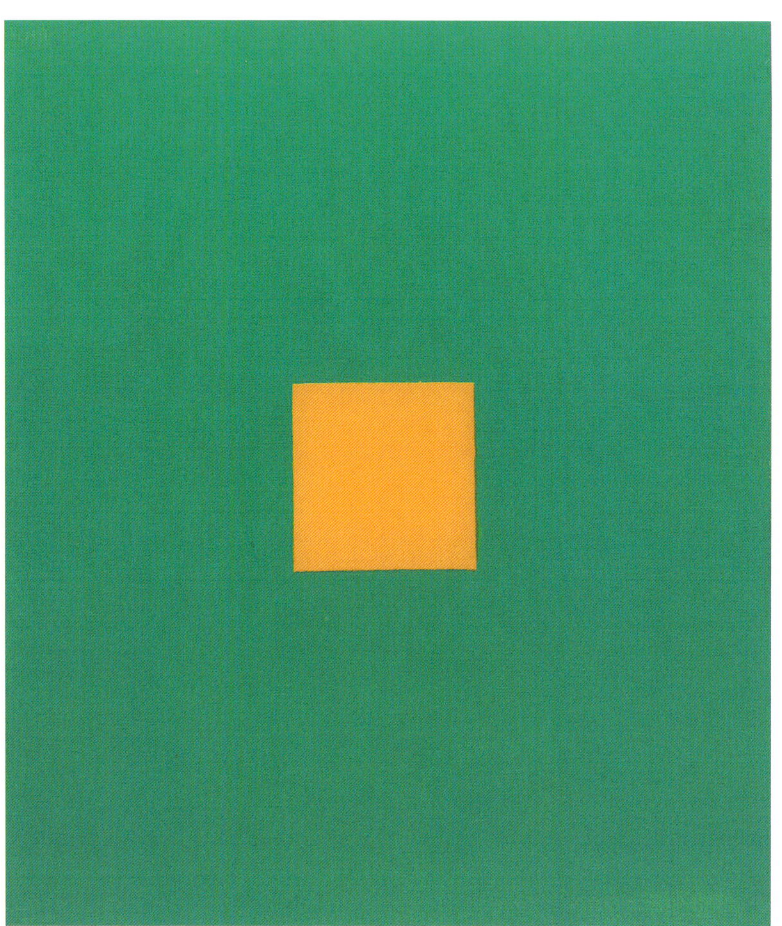

Pocket   2005
oil on canvas 76.5 x 66 cm

Enter   2004
oil on canvas   152.5 x 137.3 cm

Diverge   2005
oil on canvas 168 x 152 cm

Diverge (2)   2005
oil on canvas 168 x 152 cm

Flux (7)   2004
oil on canvas 137 x 122 cm

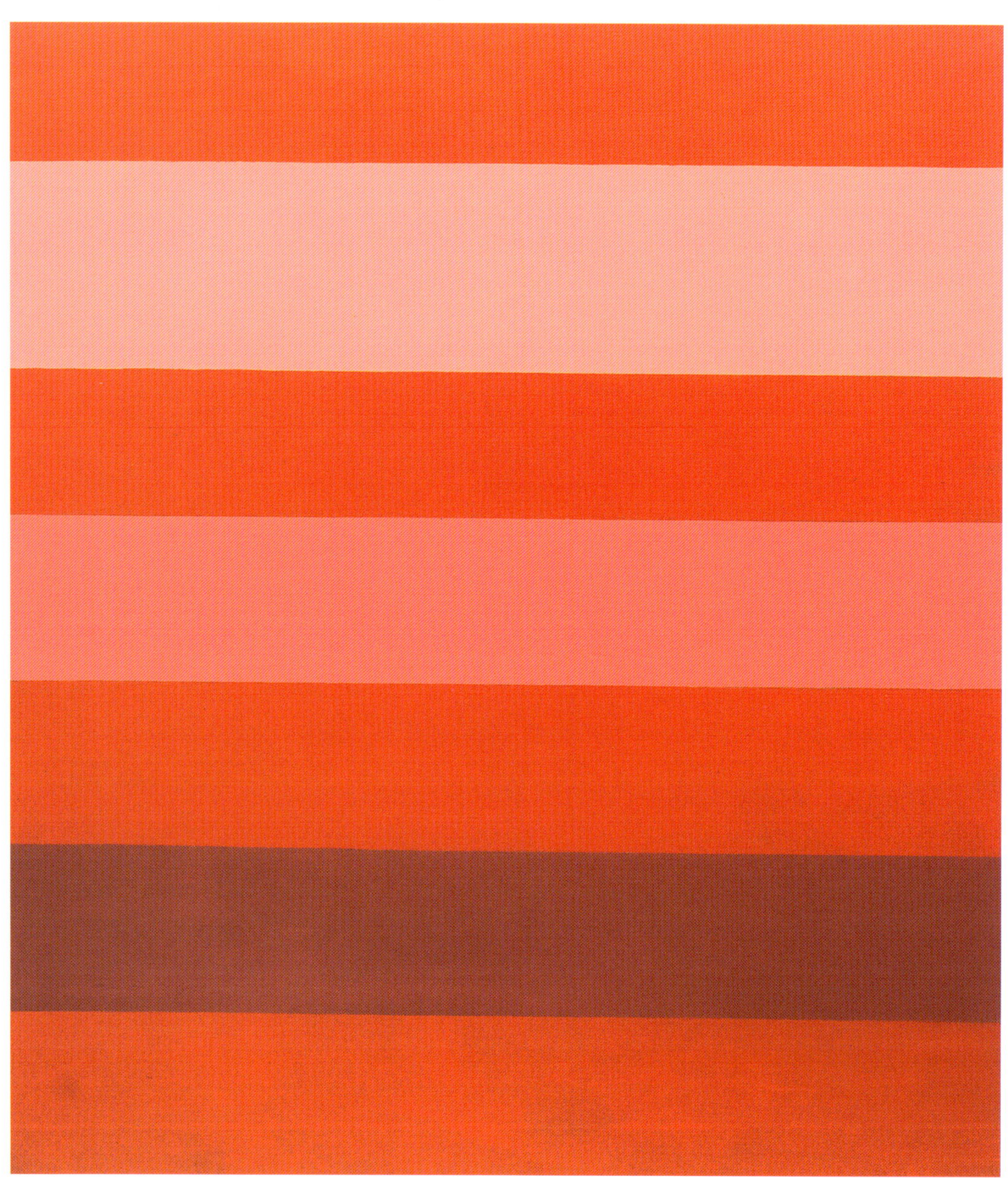

Two To Three   2005
oil on canvas   137 x 122 cm

Blink   2005
oil on canvas 137 x 122 cm

Blink (2) 2005
oil on canvas   213 x 193 cm

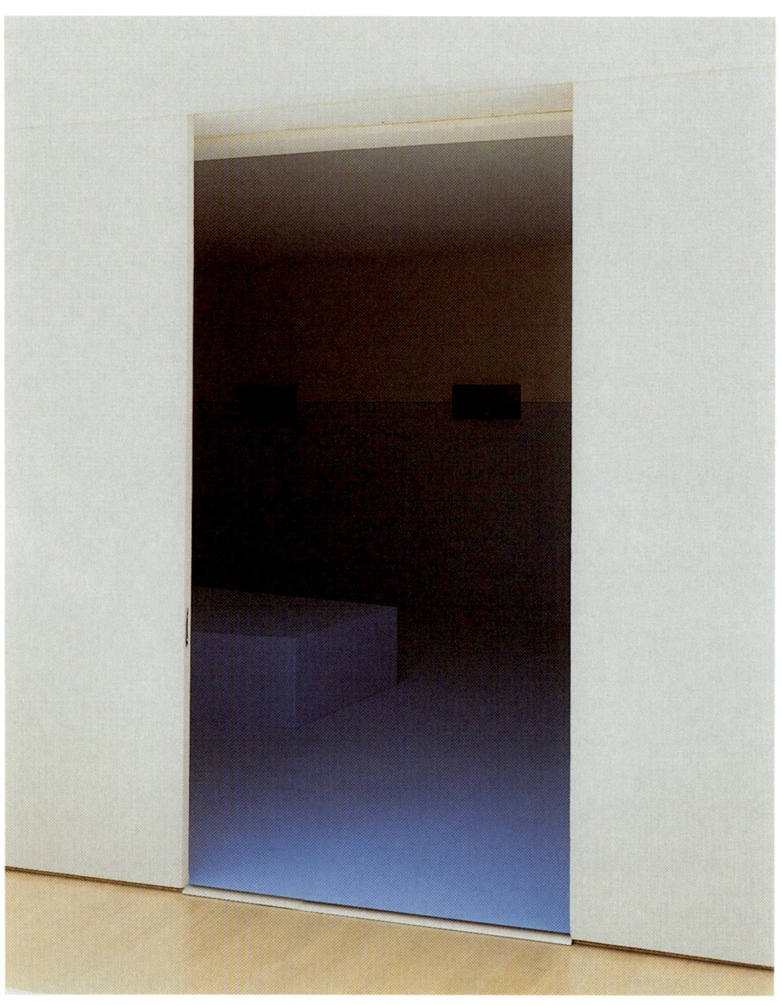

Installation: Anableps anableps/Cuatro ojos
Annely Juda Fine Art, September 2005

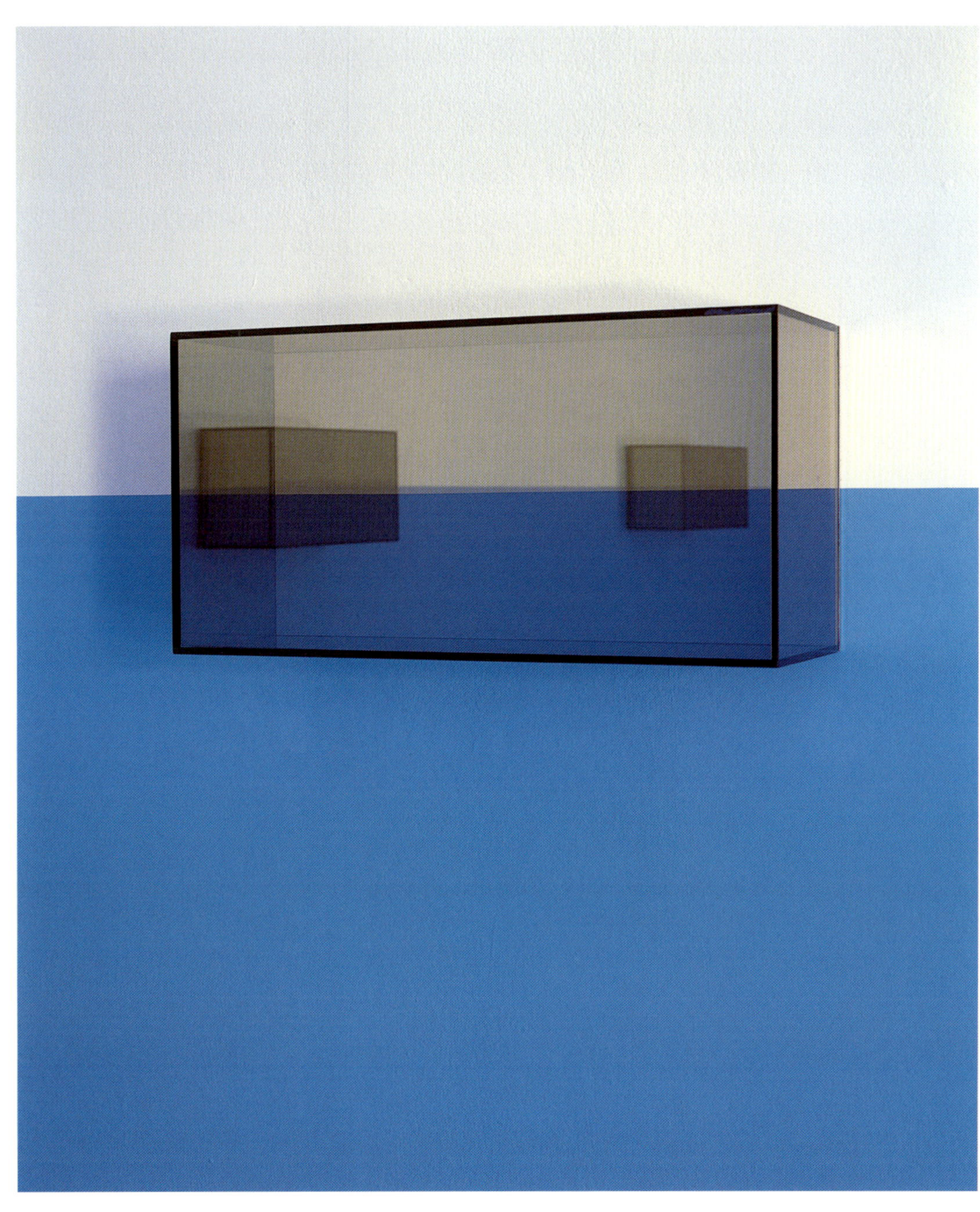

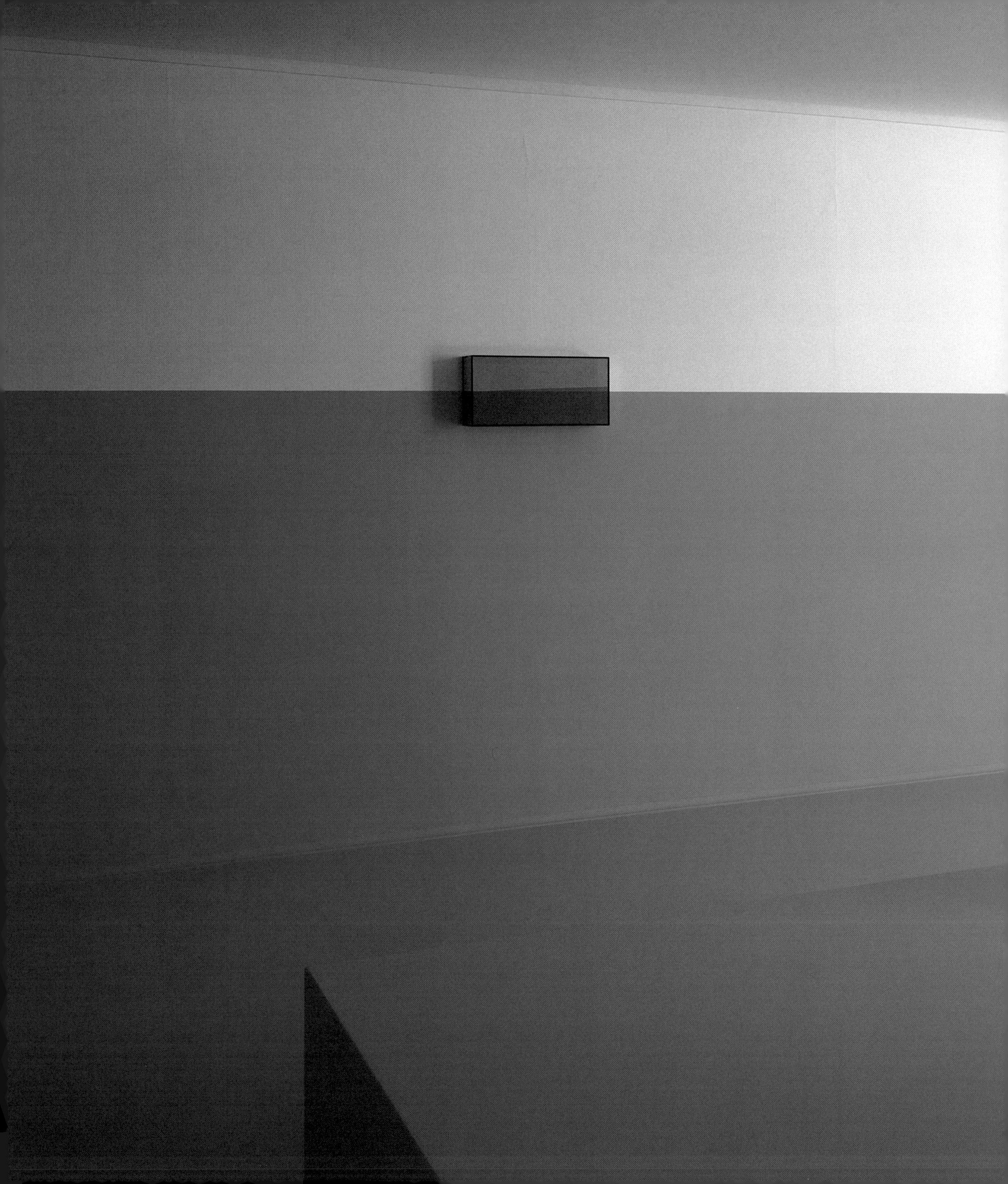

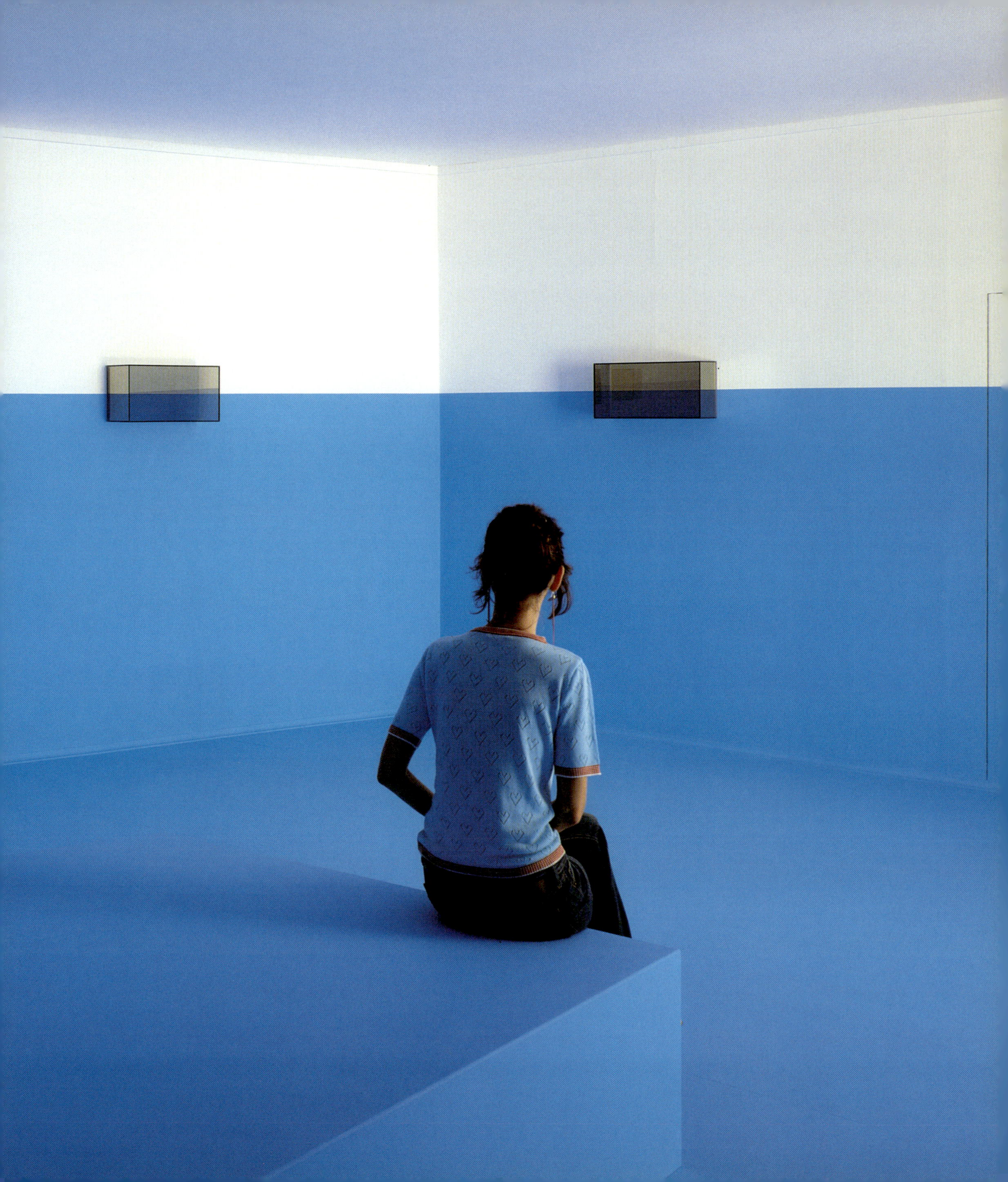

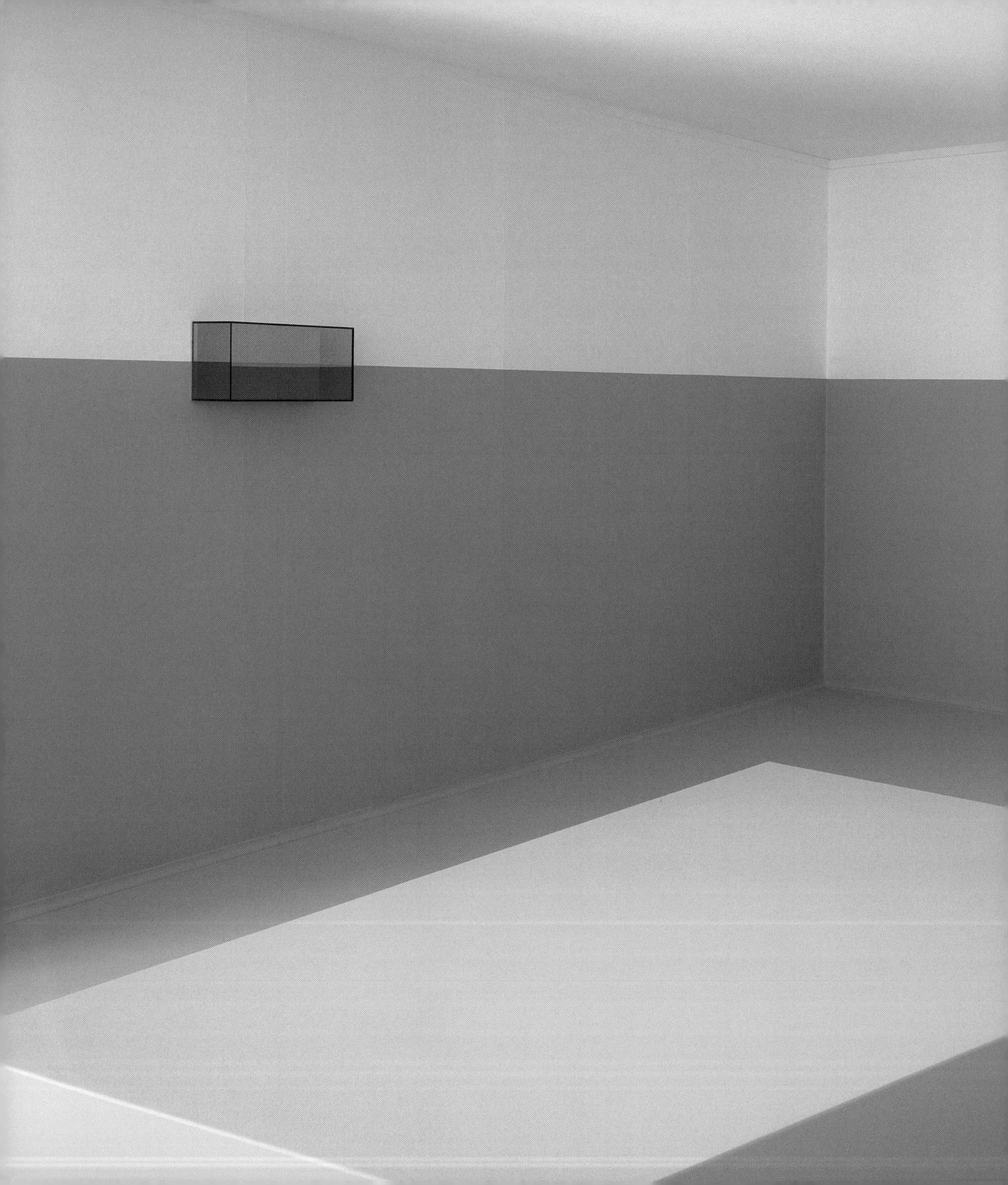

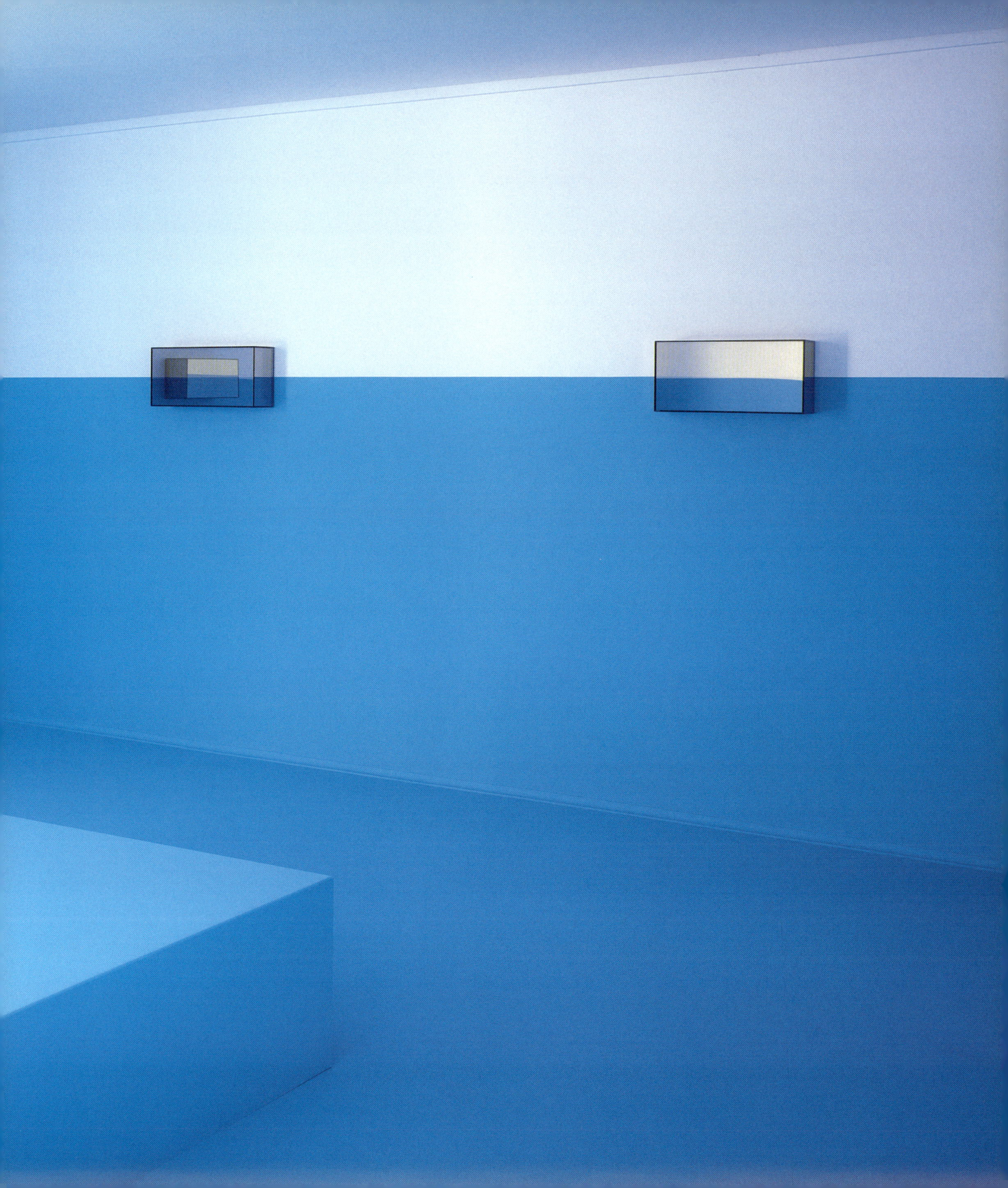

SWIMMINGPOOL

The SWIMMINGPOOL project comprises 3 experimental swimming pools.

The form, the colours and the size of the swimming pools are sculptural and they are surrounded by a 400 metre athletics track, a willow tree fence, music, natural and manmade landscape - becoming an all encompassing experience.

The SWIMMINGPOOL will be used as a sculpture theatre and ice-skating rink in the winter months.

SWIMMINGPOOL spirit merges the poetry of the wildness of nature and the strong vision of art, architecture and music. The different elements of the SWIMMINGPOOL project help the swimmer to discover new aspects of themselves.

Project Members:
Mie Miyamoto - Architect
Jonathan More (Coldcut) - Musician
Yuko Shiraishi - Artist

Location:
Stiftung Insel Hombroich
Neuss, Germany

Project Items:
Outdoor Pool: (2 months operation during summer as swimming pool)
Adult Pool 1: Shiny black, blue, tiled: 30m x 20m x 2.5m
Adult Pool 2: Mirror tiled: 75m x 4.8m x 4.2m
Kids Pool: Multi-colour, tiled: 17m in diameter x 0.5m
Surface: Berge, tiled concrete surface pebbles on concrete surface
400m Athletics Track
Café
Changing Room
Willow Fence: for cleaning water
Trees: Providing shade
Chairs
Music: MP3 Player, waterproof = (music, swimming pool, complaint. Talk/ Instruction.)
Solar Power
Locker

willow fence
water ditch. w: 2m
cafe
interior:wood, exterior: tile
l:9m x w:7m x h:6m
slope
shower
adult pool 1
shinay black+blue tile
l:30m x w:20m x d:2.5m
free
to provide shade
shower
adult pool 2
sky blue tile
l:75m x w:4.8m x d:4.2m
cafe
interior:wood, exterior: tile
l:7.5m x w:6m x h:5m
child pool
multi colour tile
17m in diameter & d: 0.6m
changind room / locker
l:24m x w:9m x d:4m
gate
MP3 player pick-up
l:10m x w:5m x d:4m
truck
l: 400m, 8 lanes

Pool : Plan

0 1   3   10   20m
scale= 1:500 (A3)

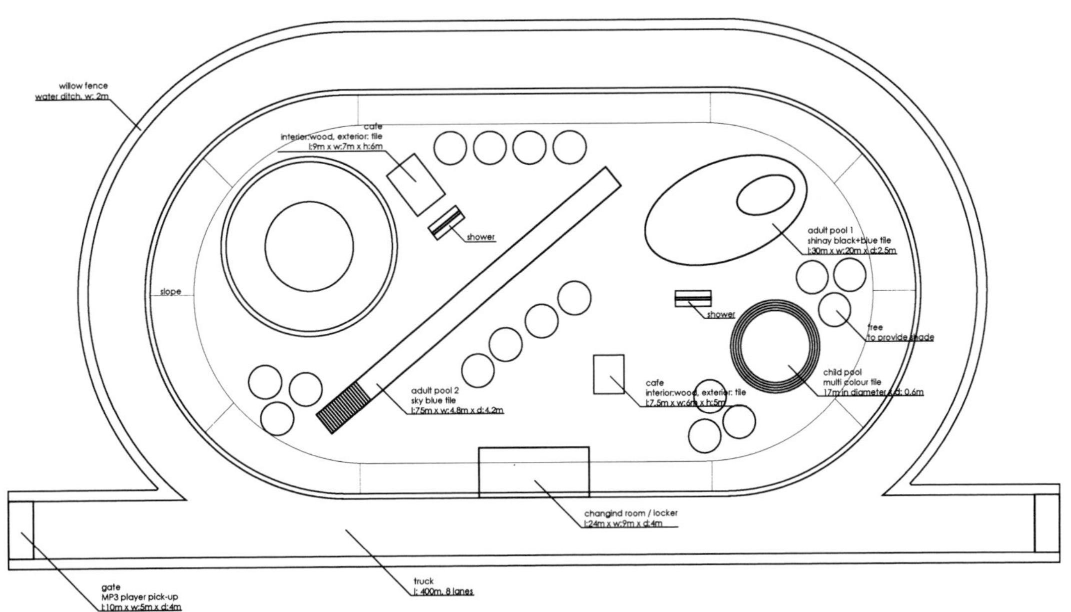

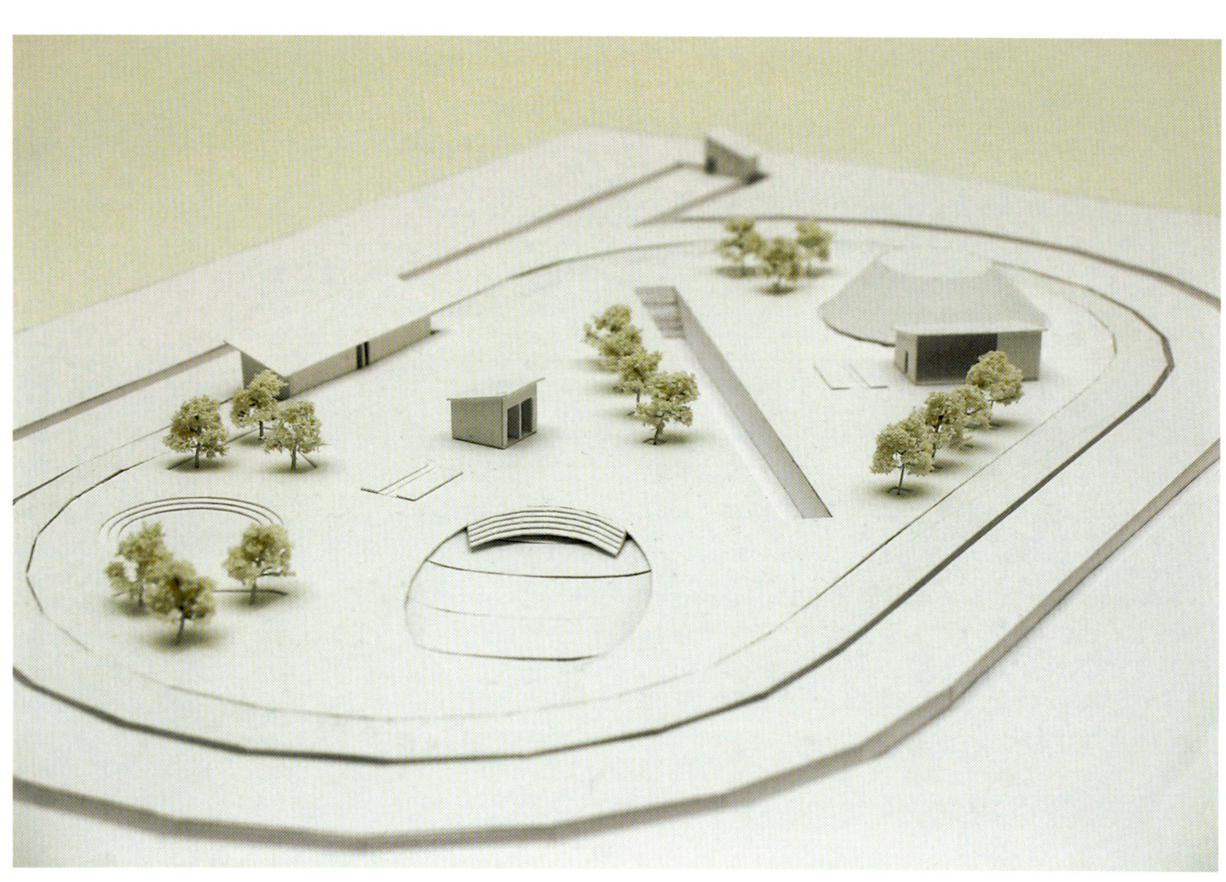

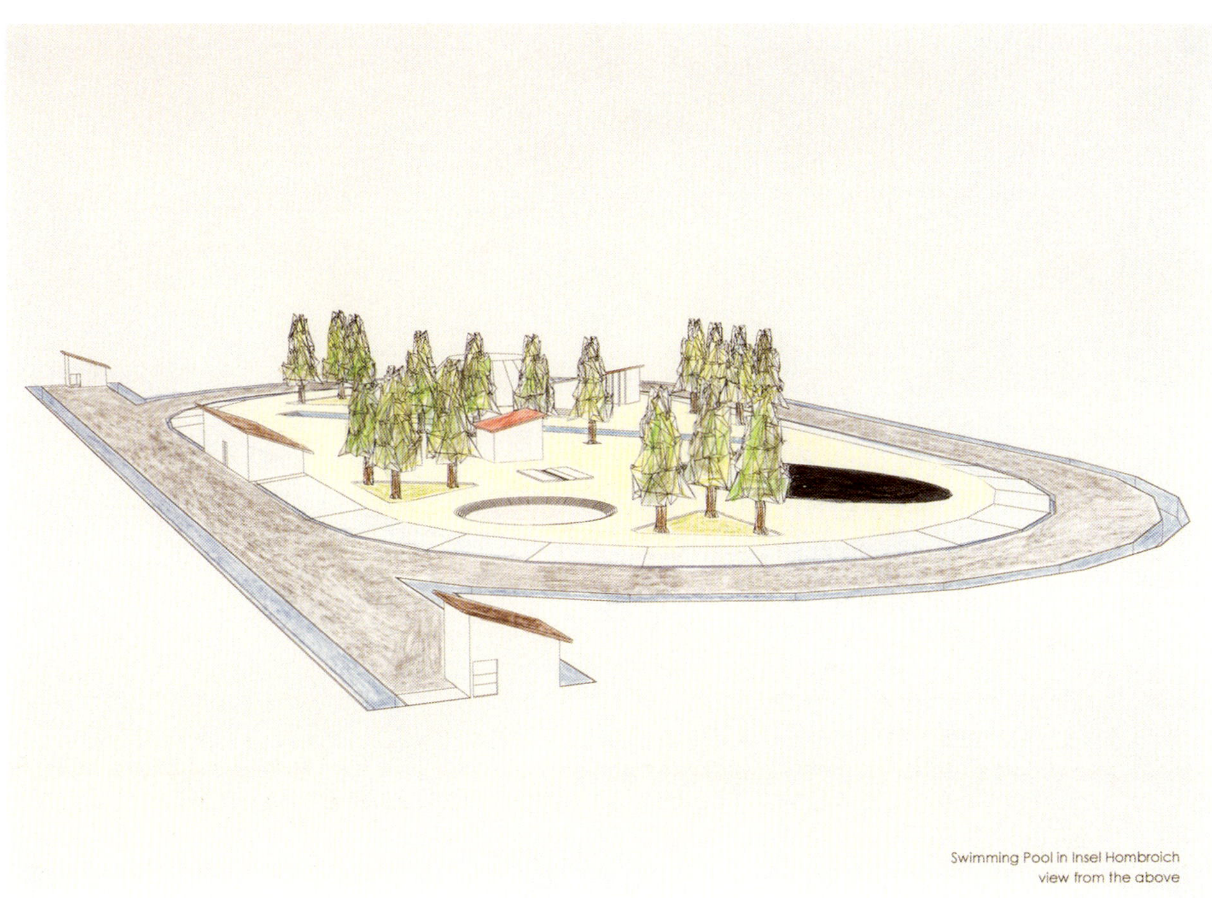

Swimming Pool in Insel Hombroich
view from the above

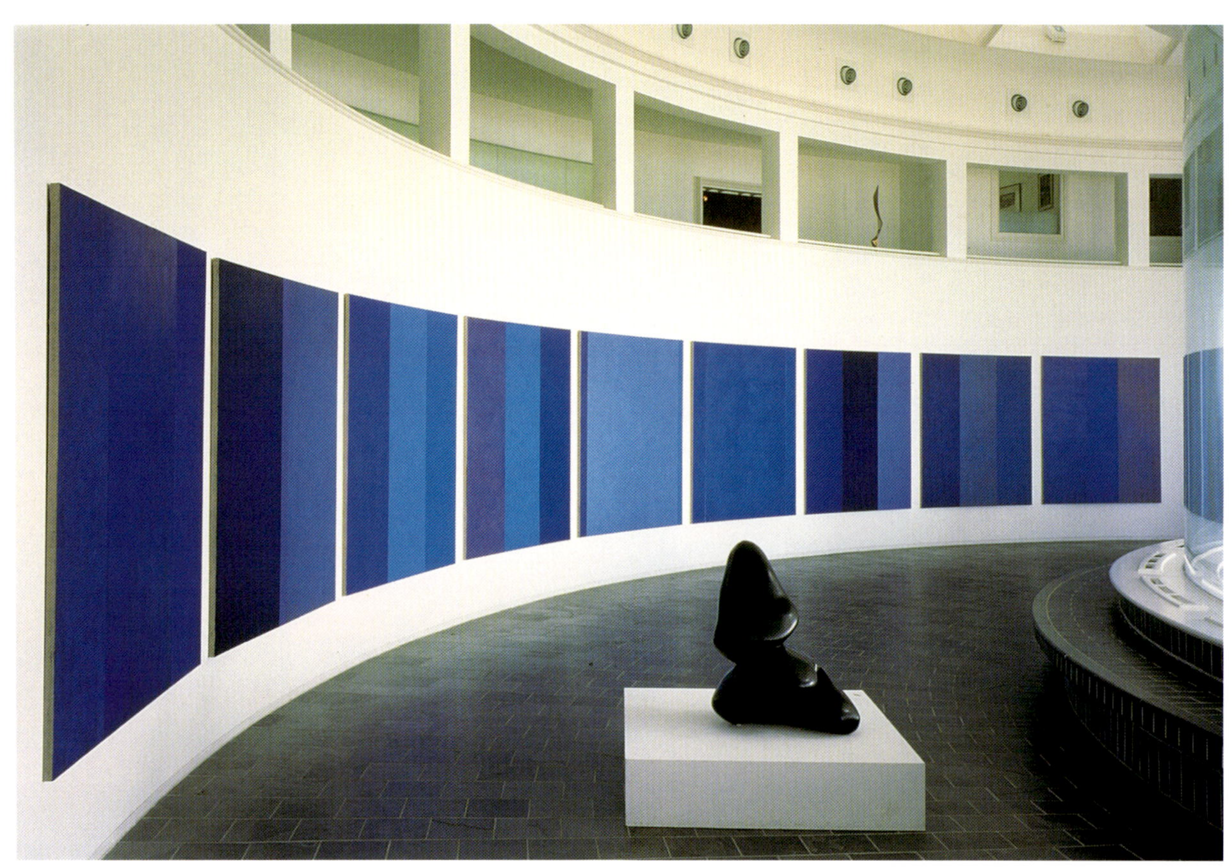

Installation of **Blue Deference 1999**, oil on canvas, 24 parts, at Tate Gallery, St Ives, 1999

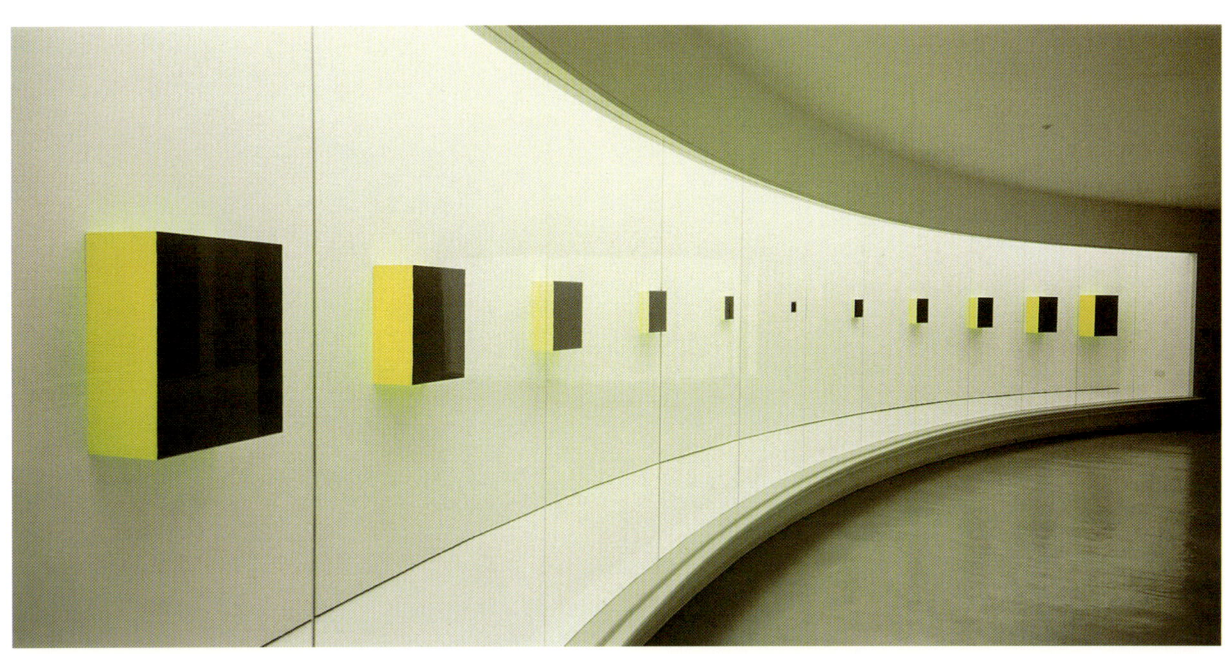

Installation of **Eclipse 1999,** oil on canvas, 11 parts, at Tate Gallery, St Ives, 1999

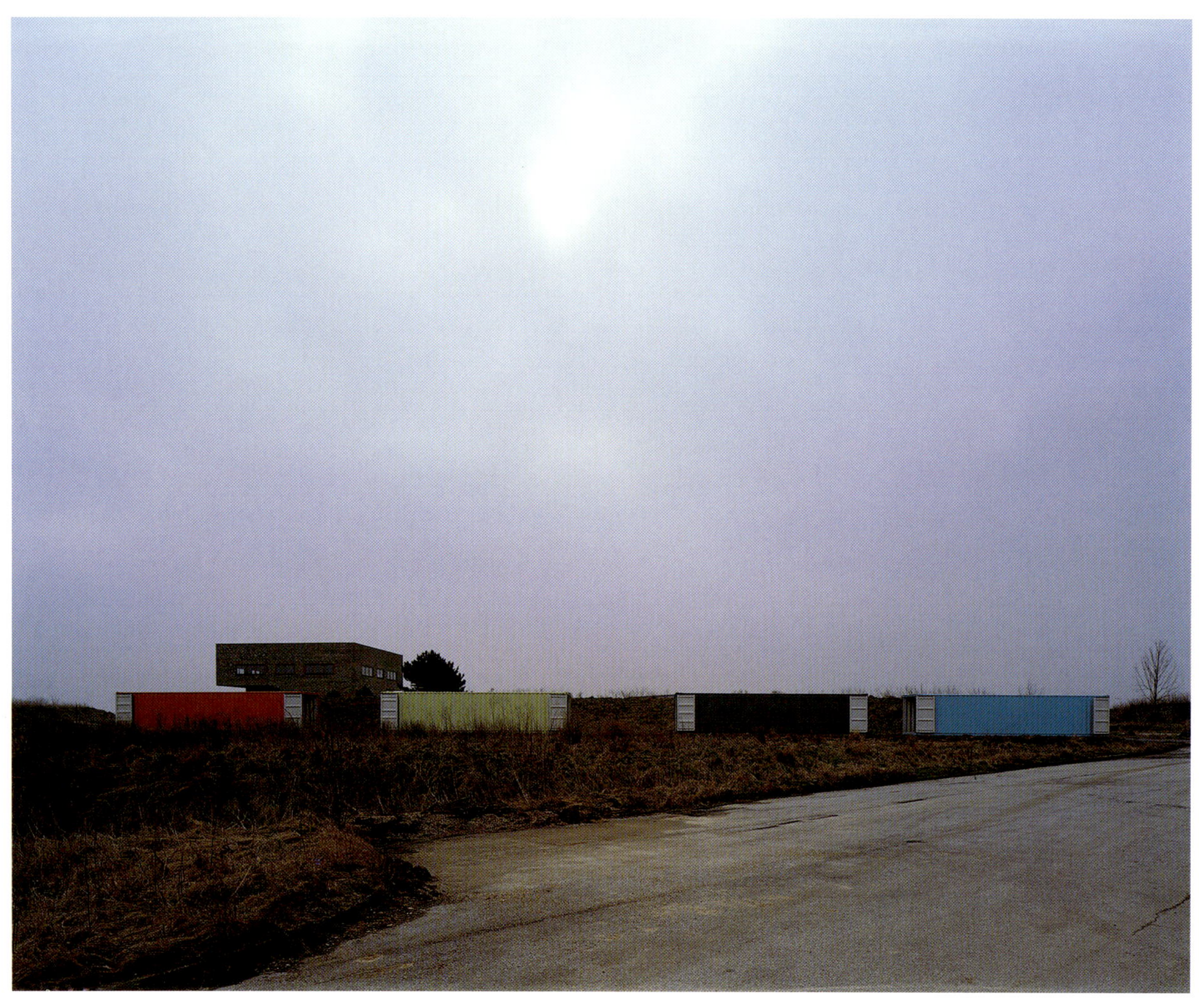

Painted container installation at Field Institute Hombroich, Stiftung Insel Hombroich Museum, Neuss, Germany, 2001

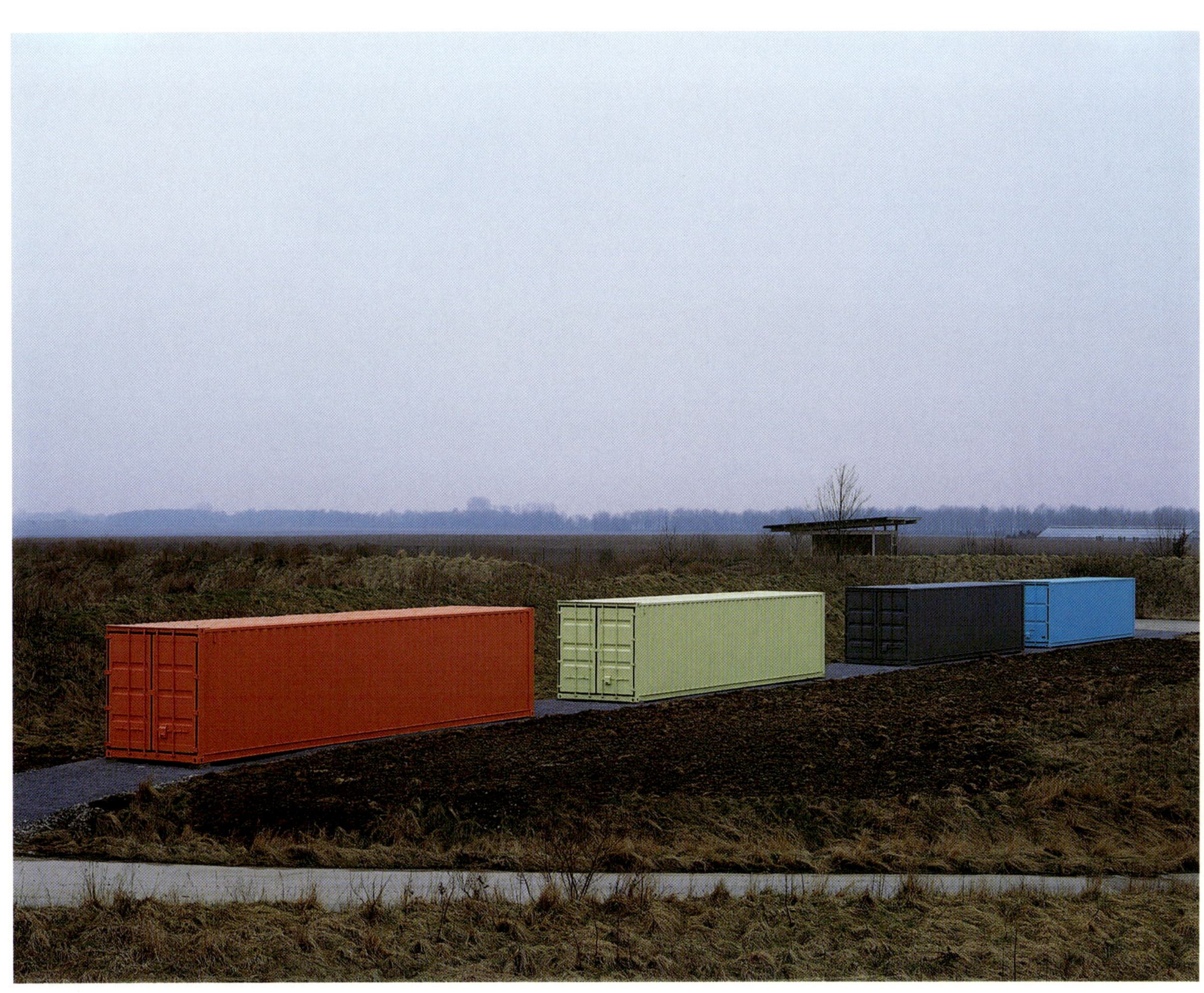

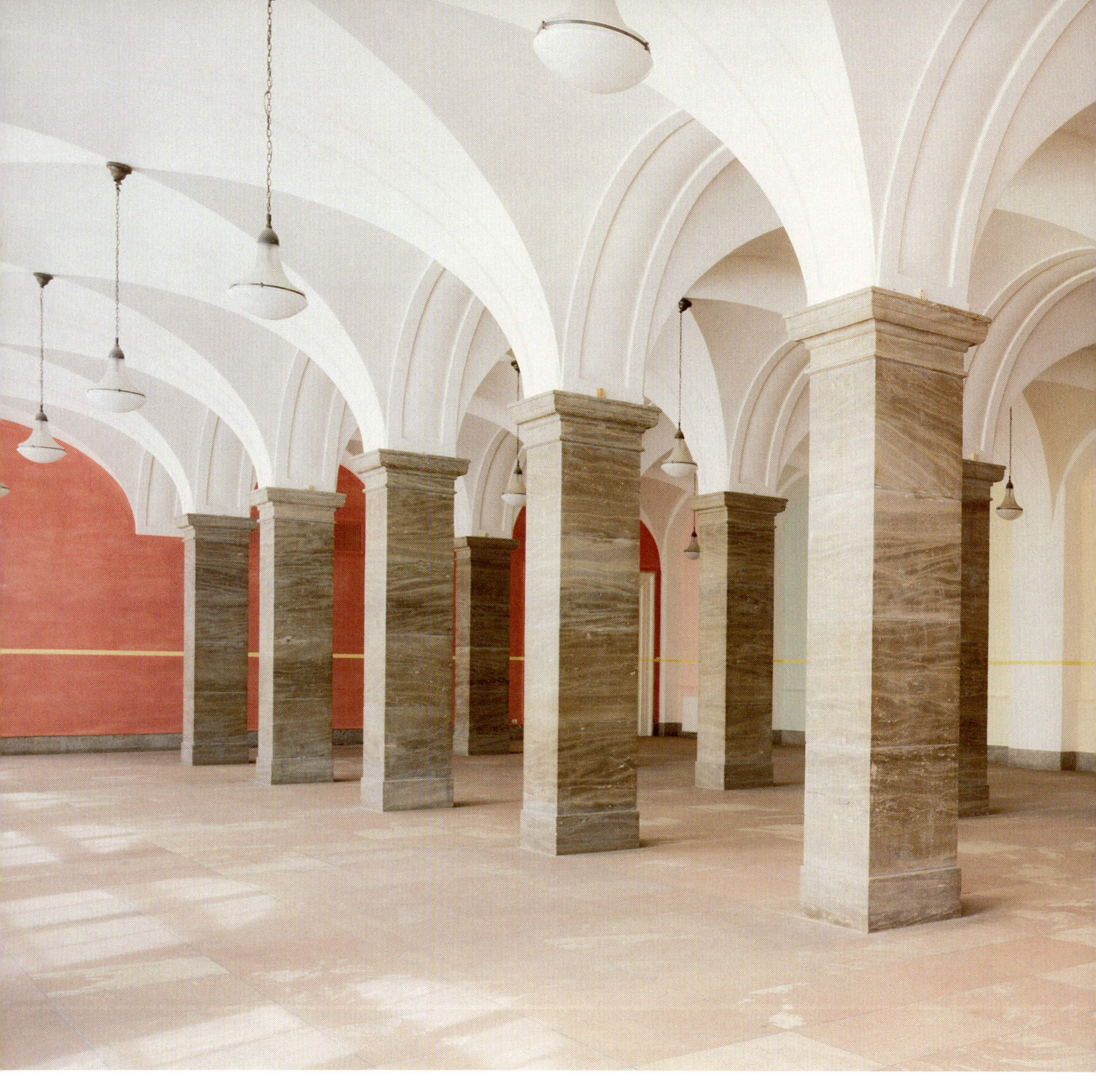

Installation at Museum Wiesbaden, 2002

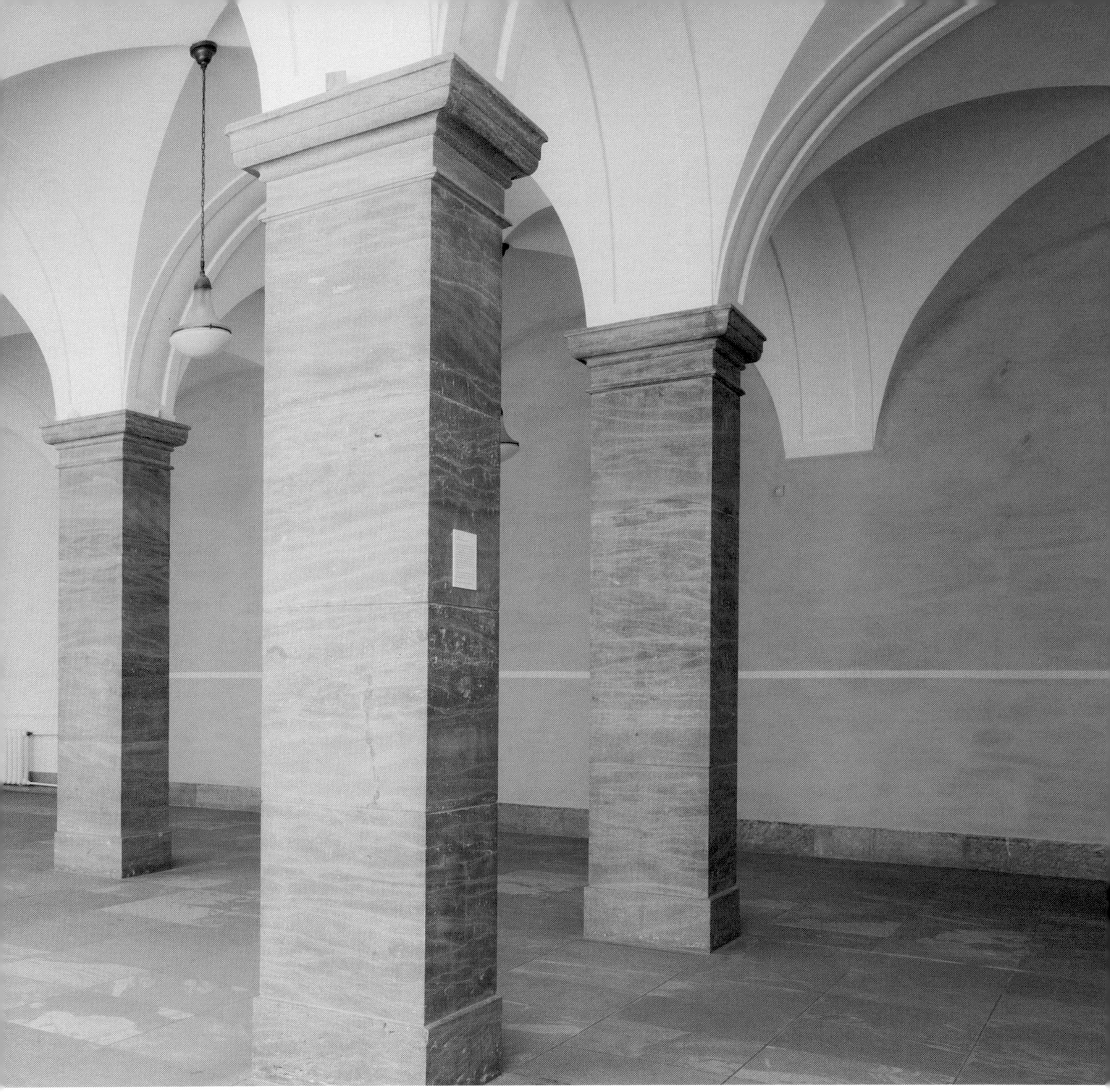

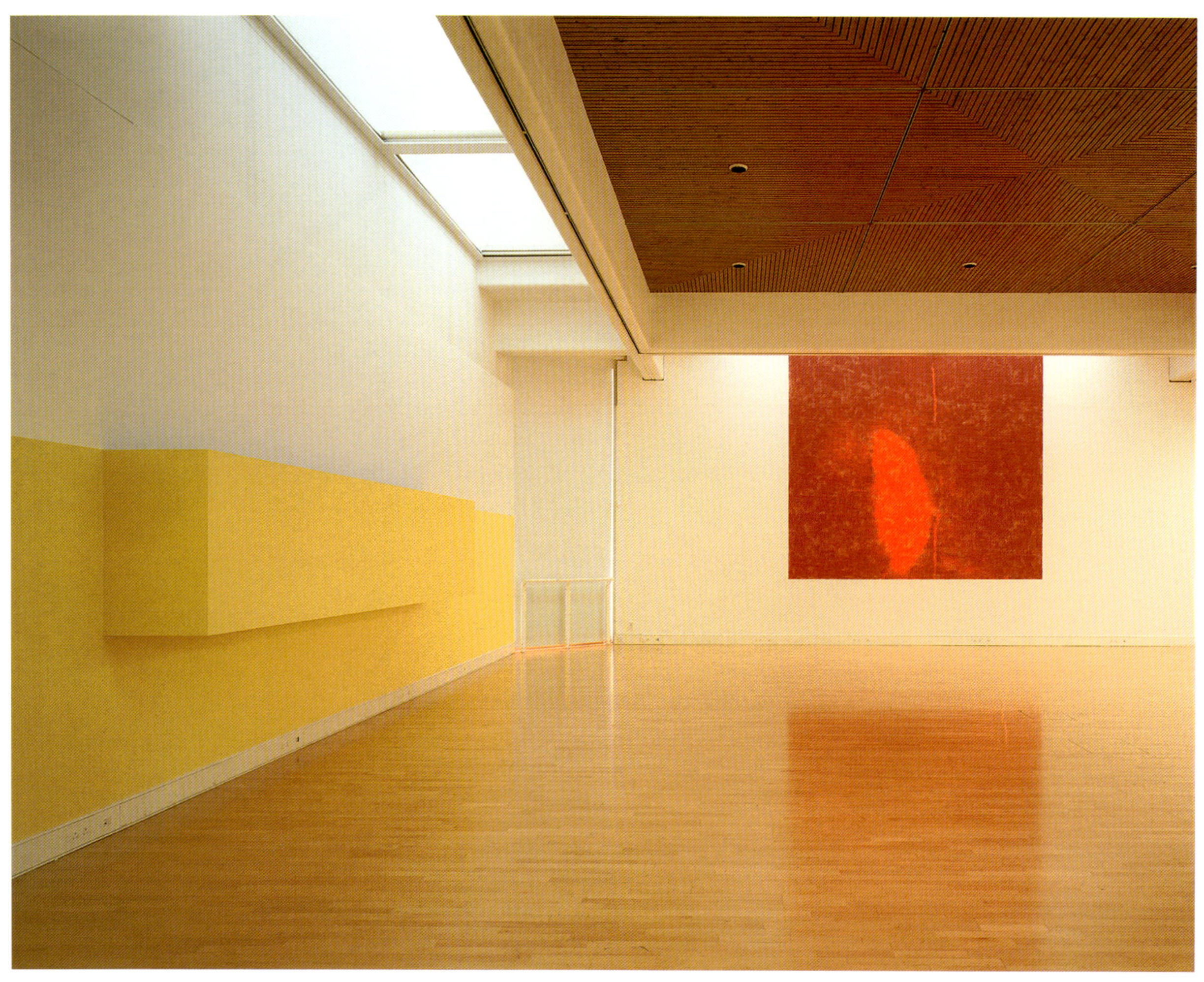

Installation at Mead Gallery, Warwick Arts Centre, Coventry, 2002

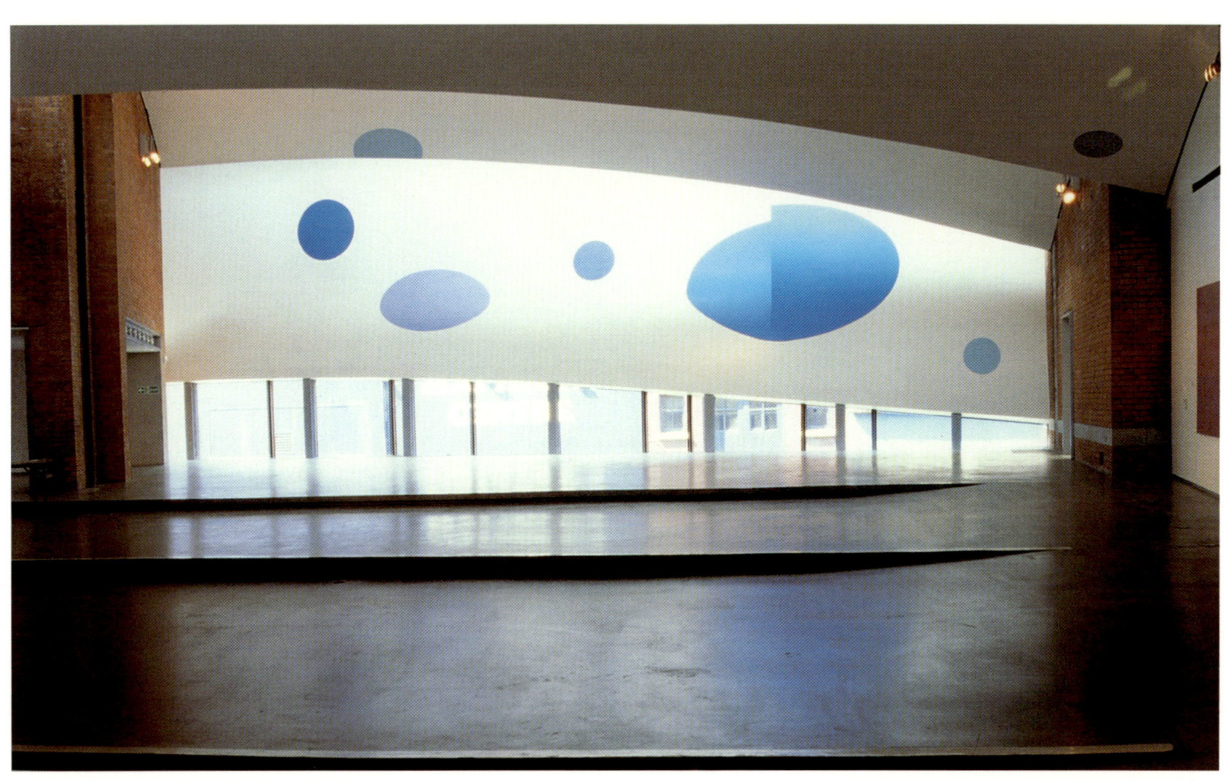

Painted wall installation, Crawford Municipal Art Gallery, Cork, 2003

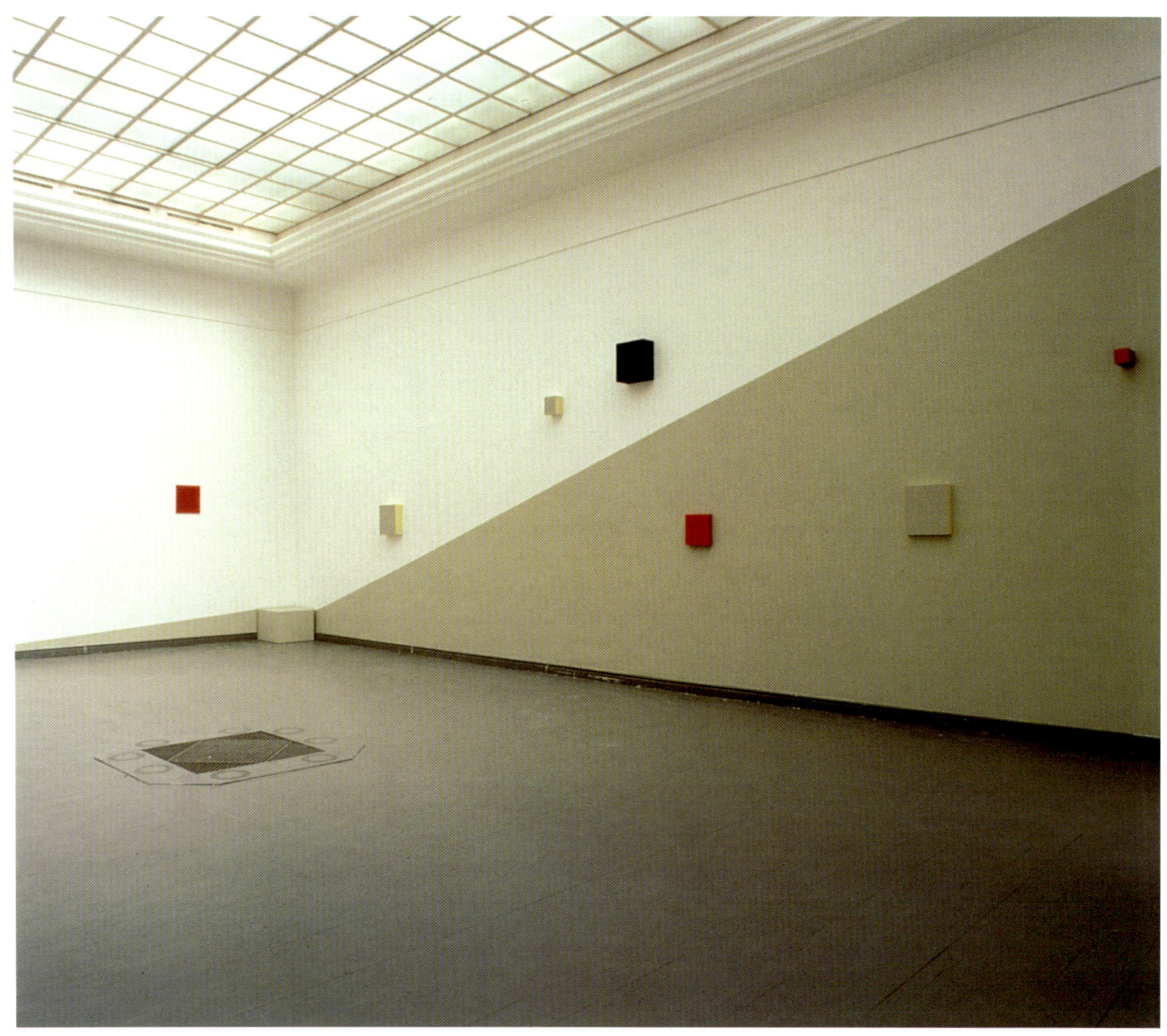

Installation at Mûcsarnok, Budapest, 2002

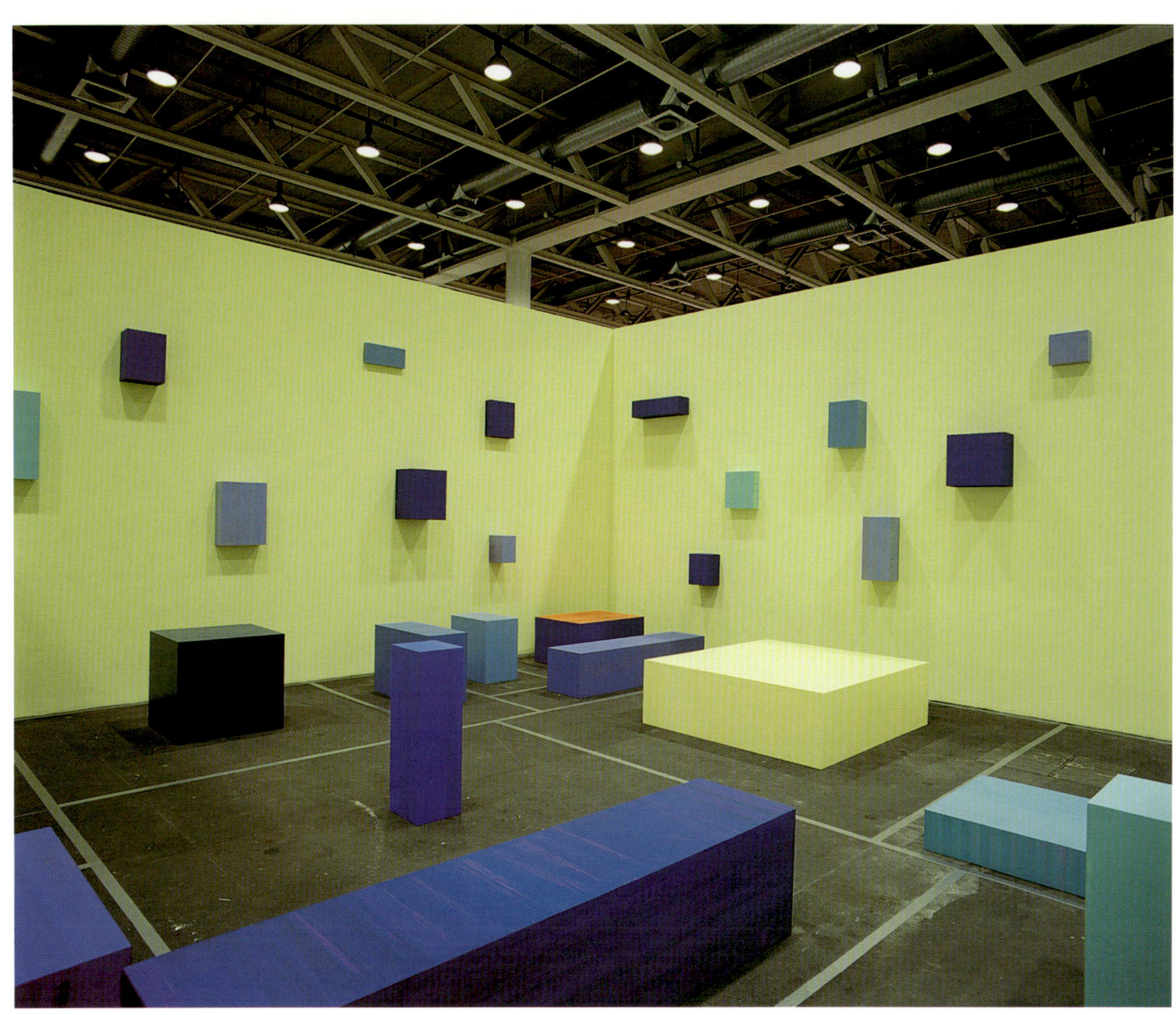

Installation at Art Unlimited, Basel, 2003

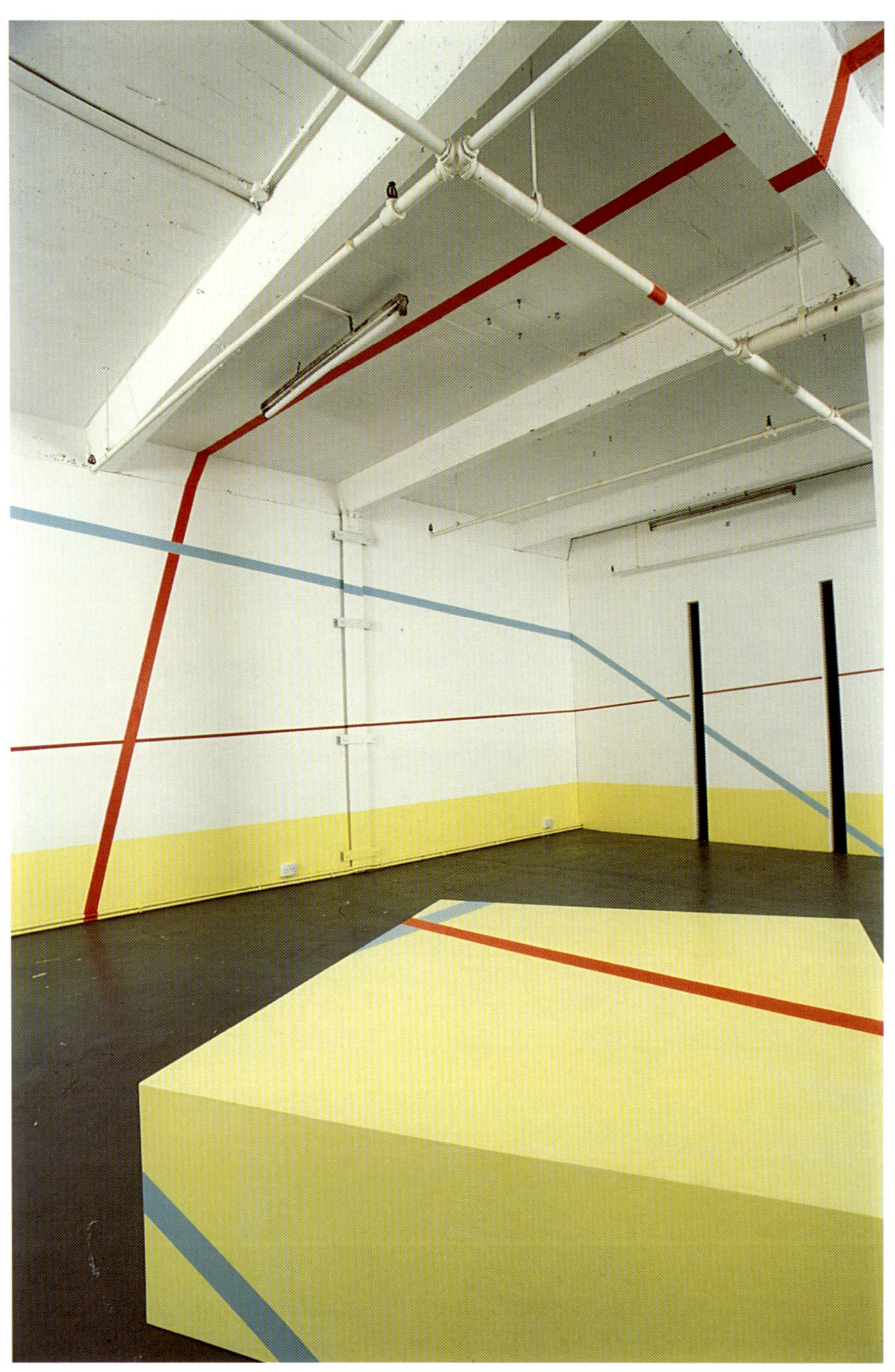

Installation at Waygood Gallery, Newcastle, 2004

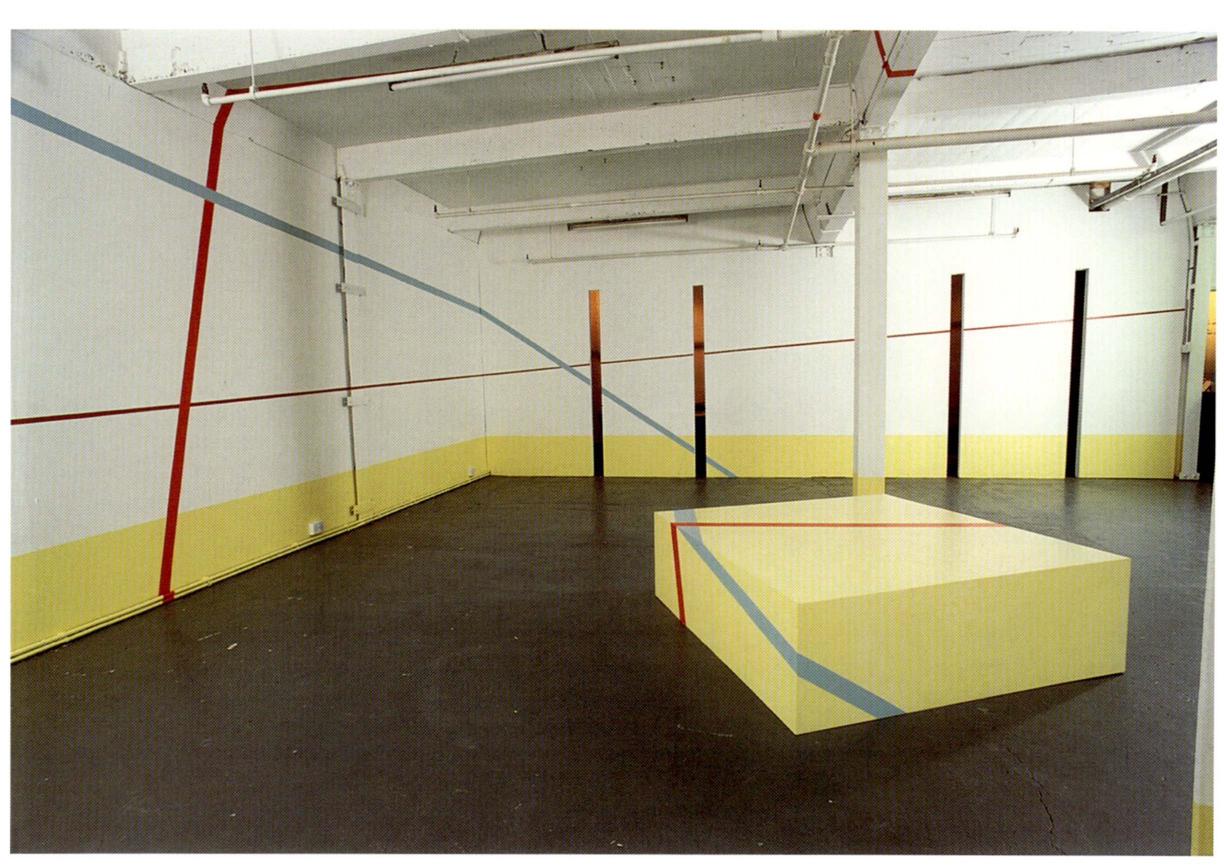

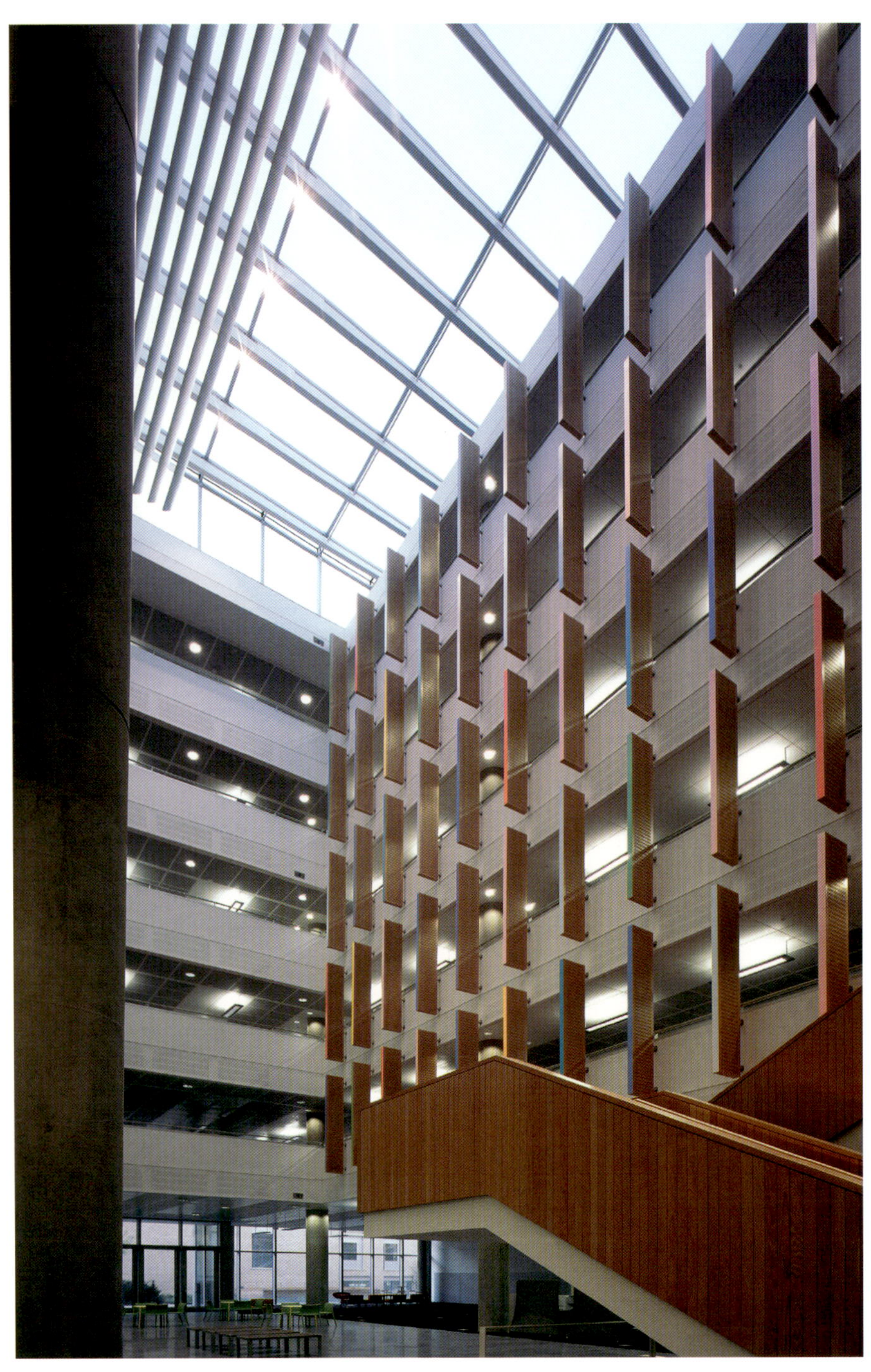

Atrium, BBC Media Centre, White City, London, 2004

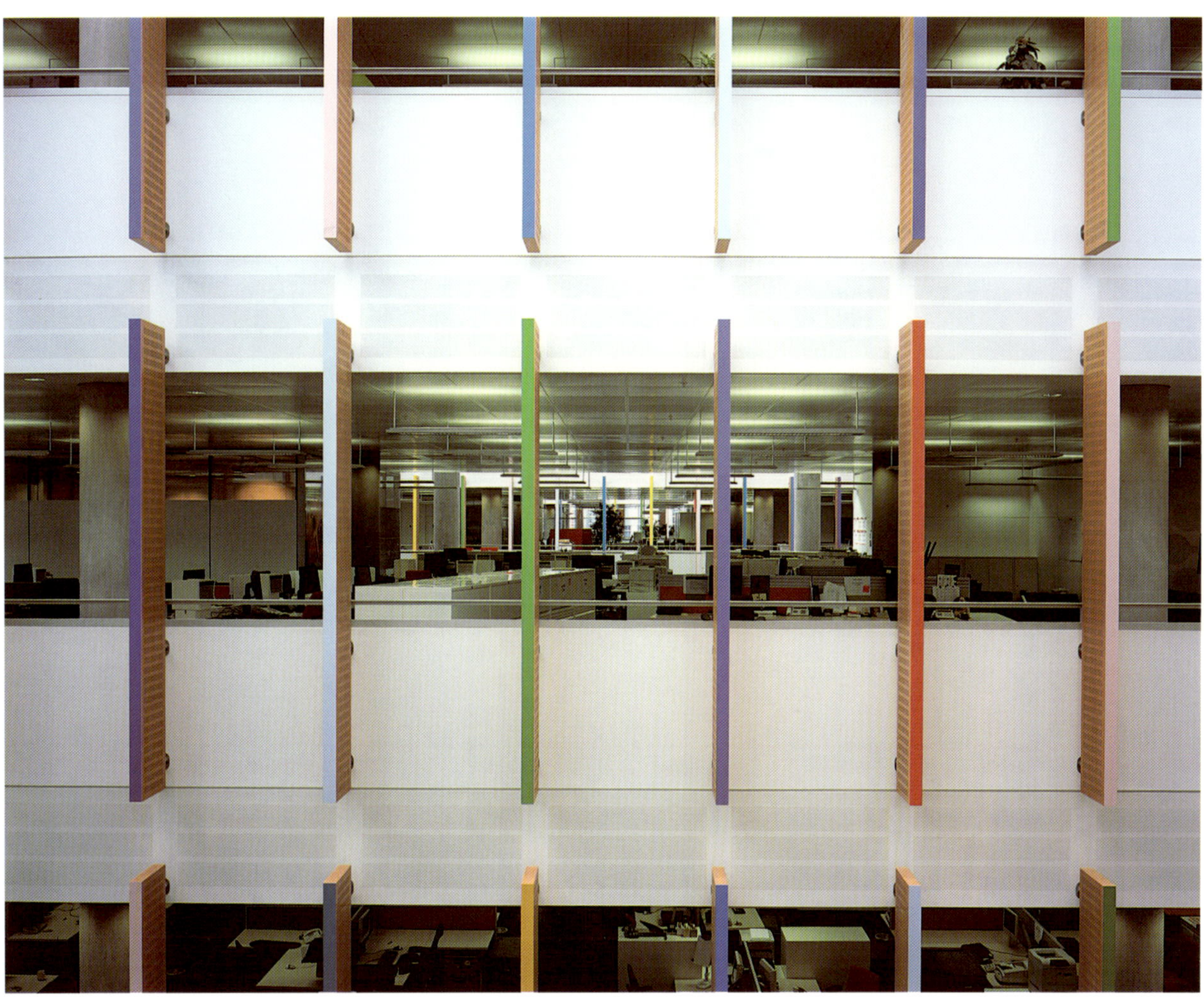

Atrium, BBC Media Centre, White City, London, 2004

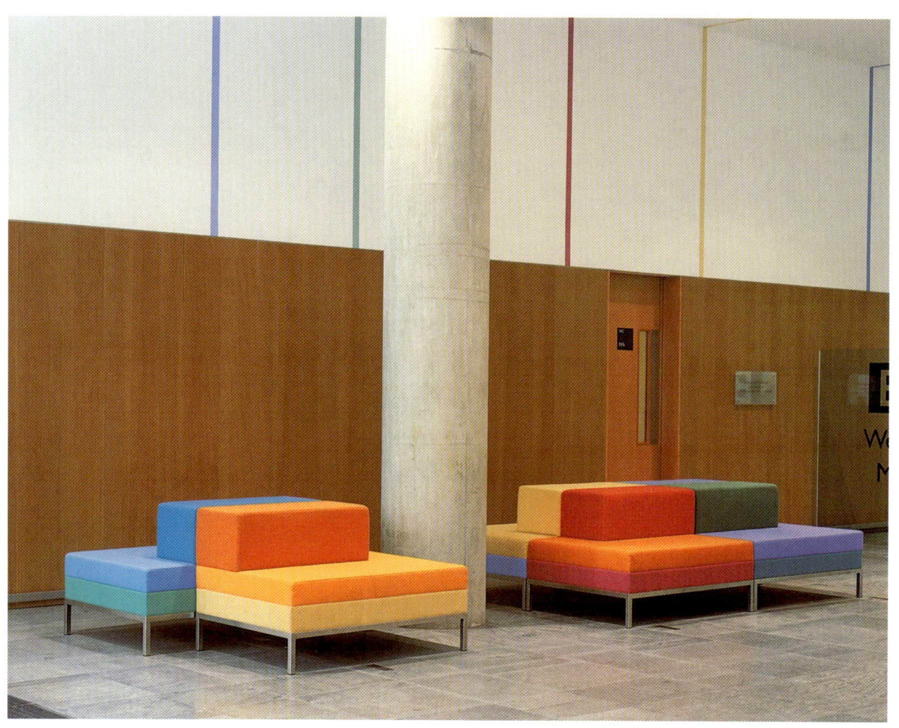

Reception area, BBC Media Centre, White City, London, 2004

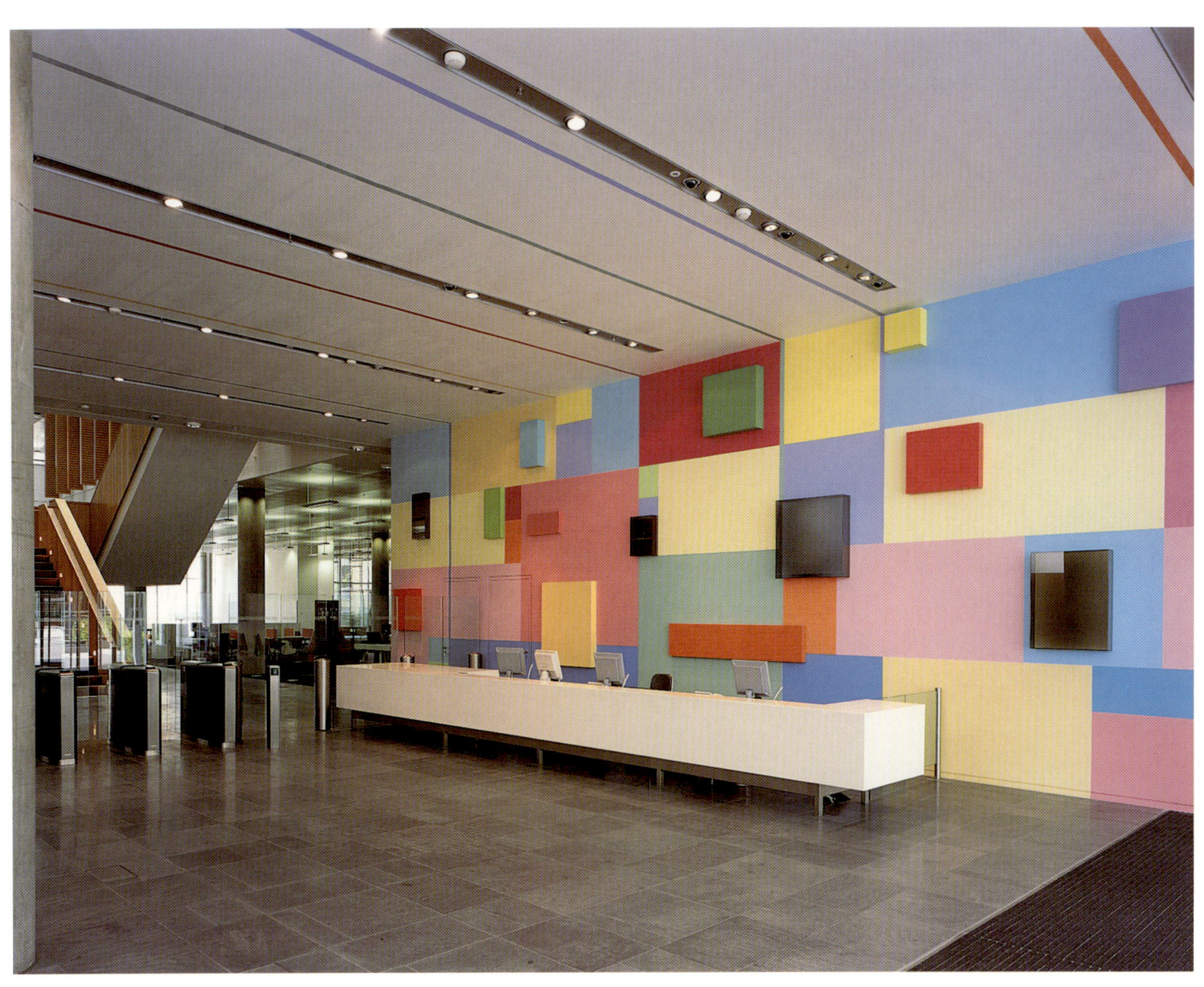

Reception area, BBC Media Centre, White City, London, 2004
Overleaf: toilet areas, BBC Media Centre, White City, London, 2004

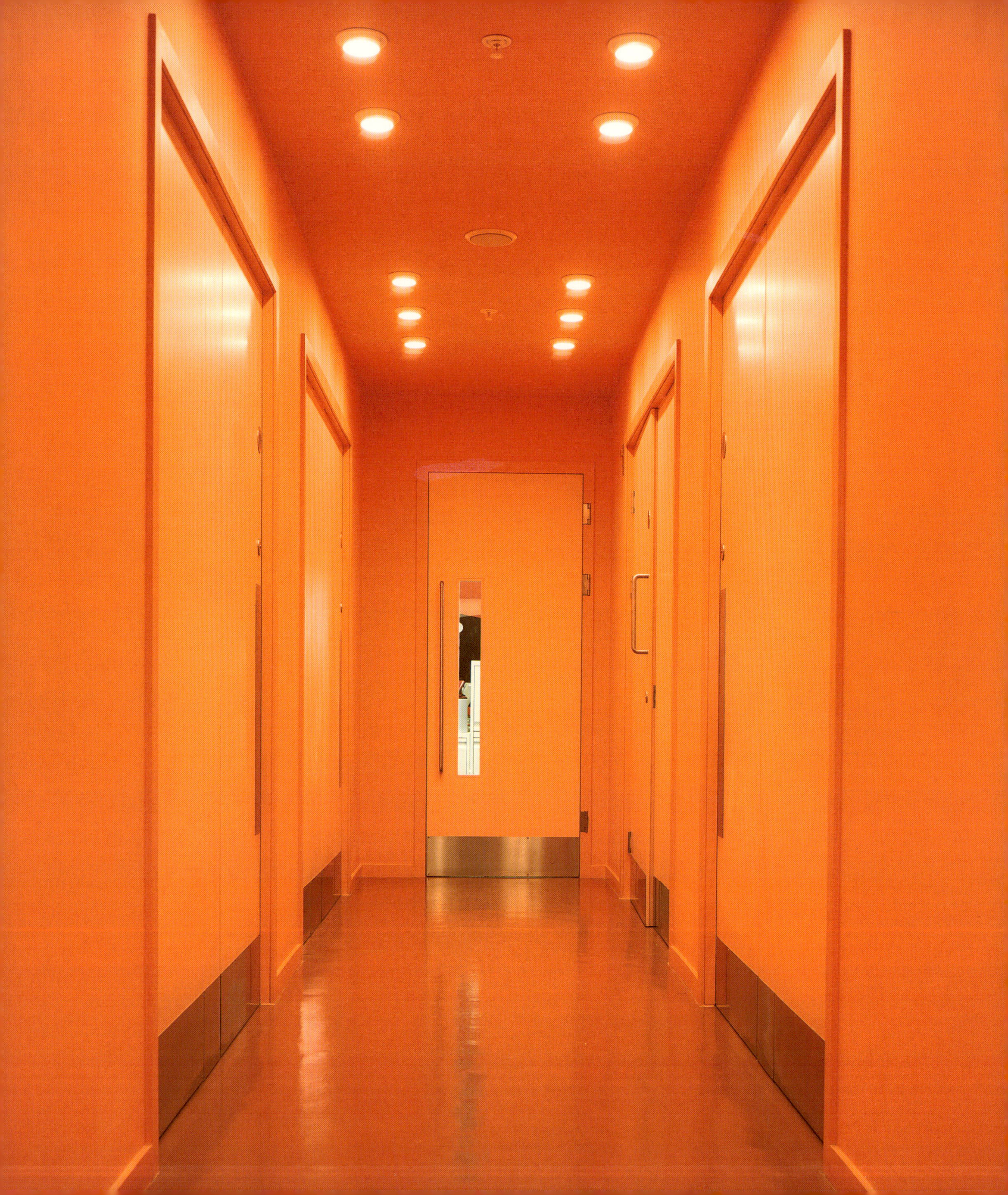

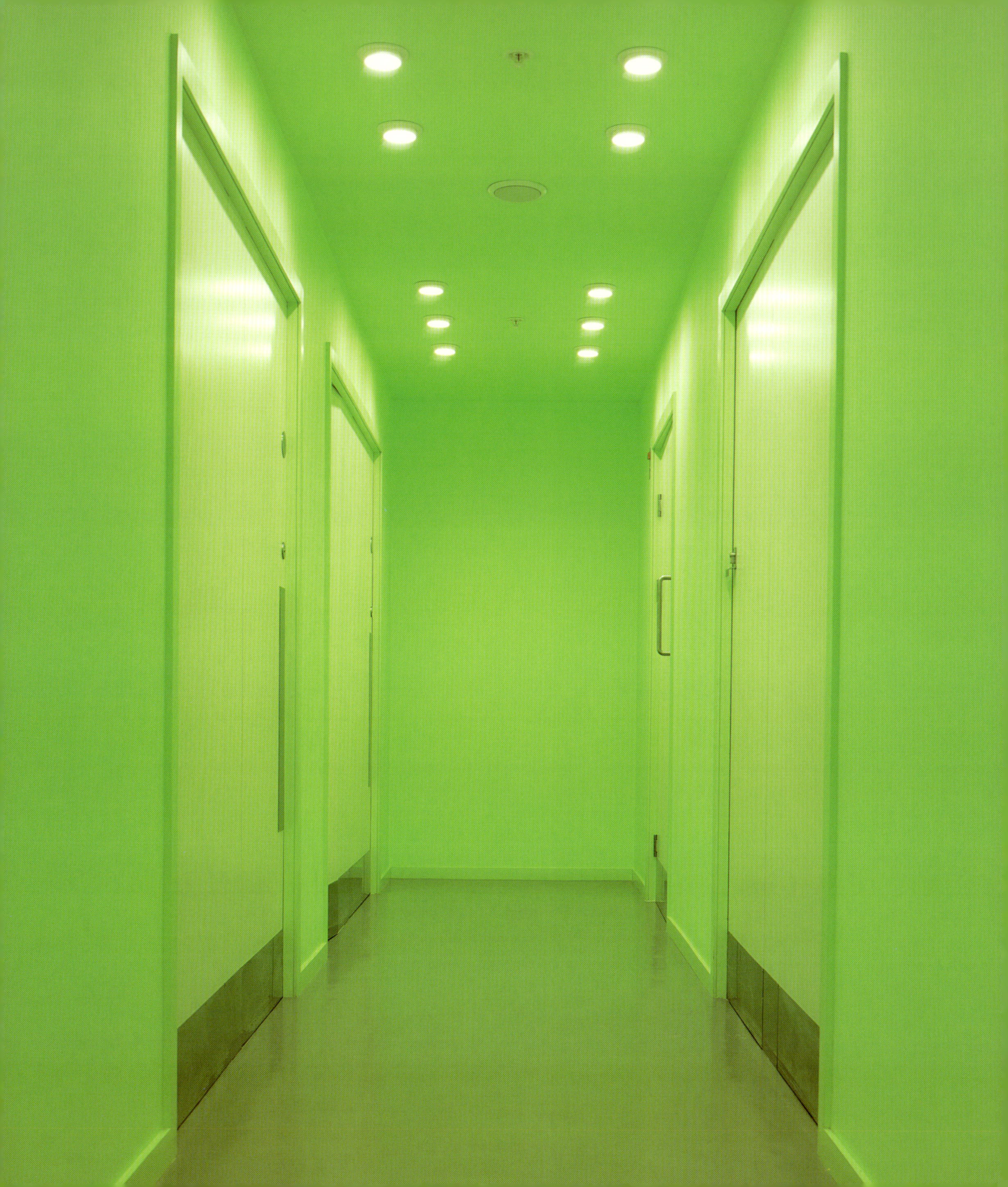

BIOGRAPHY

1956   Born Tokyo
1974-76   Lived in Vancouver, Canada
1978-81   Chelsea School of Art, BA
1981-82   Chelsea School of Art, MA

Lives and works in London

Selected one-person exhibitions

1988   Edward Totah Gallery, London
1989   Shigeru Yokota Gallery, Tokyo, Japan
1990   Galerie Konstruktiv Tendens, Stockholm, Sweden
Edward Totah Gallery, London
Artsite, Bath
1991   Cairn Gallery, Nailsworth
1992   Shigeru Yokota Gallery, Tokyo, Japan
Edward Totah Gallery, London
1994   Galerie Konstruktiv Tendens, Stockholm, Sweden
1996   Galerie Hans Mayer, Düsseldorf, Germany
Focus, Experimental Art Foundation, Adelaide, Australia
1997   Galerie Konstruktiv Tendens, Stockholm, Sweden
Shigeru Yokota Gallery, Tokyo, Japan
Juxtapositions, Annely Juda Fine Art, London
1998   Ernst Museum, Budapest, Hungary
1999   Nancy Hoffman Gallery, New York, USA
As Dark as Light, Tate Gallery, St Ives, Cornwall

2000   Galerie Konstruktiv Tendens, Stockholm, Sweden
2001   *Assemble - Disperse*, Annely Juda Fine Art, London
Shigeru Yokota Gallery, Tokyo, Japan
2002   *Infinite Line, Die unendliche Linie*, Museum Wiesbaden, Germany
Episode, Mead Gallery, Warwick Arts Centre, University of Warwick, Coventry
2003   *Episode*, travelled to Leeds City Art Gallery
Yuko Shiraishi – There and Back, Crawford Municipal Art Gallery, Cork
Tuesday is cerise, Waygood Gallery, Newcastle
2005   *Temperature: Installation, Project and Painting*, Annely Juda Fine Art, London

Projects

2001-   FIH: Field Institute Hombroich (with Tadashi Kawamata, Katsuhito Nishikawa), Stiftung Insel Hombroich Museum, Neuss, Germany
2001-4   BBC White City Project (with Allies & Morrison), London
2005   Jiundou Hospital, Tokyo, Japan
Swimmingpool (with Mie Miyamoto, Jonathan More - Coldcut), Stiftung Insel Hombroich Museum, Neuss, Germany

Selected group exhibitions

1980   *New Contemporaries*, ICA, London
1988   *The Presence of Painting: Aspects of British Abstraction 1957-88*, Arts Council Touring Exhibition, Mappin Art Gallery, Sheffield, Hatton Arts Gallery, Newcastle, Ikon Gallery, Birmingham
1990   *Künstlerinnen des 20. Jahrhunderts*, Museum Wiesbaden, Germany
Galerie Konstruktiv Tendens, Stockholm, Sweden
Whitechapel Open, Whitechapel Art Gallery, London
1991   *Double Take*, American Japan Art Association, New York, USA
1992   *Geteilte Bilder - Das Diptychon in der neuen Kunst*, Folkwang Museum, Essen, Germany
A Sense of Purpose, Mappin Art Gallery, Sheffield
1993   *Moving into view - Recent British Paintings*, Arts Council Touring Exhibition
Zwei Energien, Haus für Konstruktive und Konkrete Kunst, Zurich, Switzerland
Contemporary Art, Courtauld Institute, London
1994   *Unveiled*, Cornerhouse Gallery, Manchester
Jerwood Painting Prize 1994, Royal Scottish Academy, Edinburgh, Royal Academy of Arts, London
1995   *New Painting*, Arts Council Touring Exhibition
Pretext Heteronyms, Clink Street, curated by Rear Window

1996   *New Paintings from the Arts Council Collection*, Bath Museum
1997   *Pretext Heteronyms*, San Michele, Rome, Italy; Haus Bill, Zumikon, Zurich, Switzerland
1998   *Clear and Saturated*, Arti et Amicitiae, Amsterdam, The Netherlands
Immerzeit, Forum Konkrete Kunst Galerie am Fischmarkt, Erfurt, Germany
1999   *Geometrie als Gestalt*, Neue Nationalgalerie, Berlin, Germany
Vendégjáték, Ludwig Museum Budapest, Hungary
2000   *Blue: Borrowed and New*, The New Art Gallery, Walsall
Grau ist nicht Grau, Galerie Gisèle Linder, Basel, Switzerland
2001   *Nu Konstruktiv Tendens - efter 20ar*, Galerie Konstruktiv Tendens, Stockholm, Sweden
2002   *Colour - A Life of Its Own*, Mûcsarnok, Budapest, Hungary
2003   *Index on Colour*, Leeds City Art Gallery
Art Unlimited, Basel, Switzerland
2004   Art Scope Daimler Chrysler Japan, Daimler Chrysler, Berlin, Germany
APRIORI, Galerie Dorothea van der Koelen, Venice, Italy, Mainz, Germany
2005   Swimmingpool (with Mie Miyamoto, Jonathan More-Coldcut), FIH, Stifung Insel Hombroich Museum, Neuss, Germany

Selected public collections

Arts Council of Great Britain
British Council, London
British Government Collection, London
British Museum, London
Contemporary Art Society, London
Graphische Sammlung Albertina, Vienna, Austria
Graves City Art Gallery, Sheffield
Ludwig Museum, Budapest, Hungary
Max Bill - George Vantongerloo, Zumikon, Switzerland
McCrory Corporation, New York, USA
The National Museum of Art, Osaka, Japan
Ohara Museum, Kurashiki, Japan
Weishaupt Forum, Ulm, Germany

Selected bibliography

1988   Sarah Kent, *Time Out*, May
James Burr, *Apollo*, May
'The Presence of Painting', catalogue essay by Michael Tooby, Arts Council Touring Exhibition
'Aspects of British Abstraction 1957-1988', Mappin Art Gallery, Sheffield
Marina Vaizey, *The Sunday Times*, 11 December

1989   catalogue essay by Yuko Shiraishi, Tieerhuys Galerij, Belgium
'Abstract Connection', William Packer, *The Financial Times*, August
'Yuko Shiraishi', catalogue essay by Michel Tooby, Shigeru Gallery Tokyo

1990   Fumio Nanjyo, *Flash Art International*, March / April
'Yuko Shiraishi', catalogue essay by Margaret Garlake, Edward Totah Gallery, London
Robert MacDonald, *Time Out*, May
Mel Gooding, *Art Monthly*, July / August
Sacha Craddock, *The Guardian*, 10 October
'Künstlerinnen des 20. Jahrhunderts', catalogue essay by Sister Wendy Beckett, Museum Wiesbaden

1991   'Double Take Japan-America', catalogue essay by Michael Tooby and Akira Tatehata, Art Association, New York

1992   Janet Koplos, *Art in America*, May
'Geteilte Bilder - Das Diptychon in der neuen Kunst', catalogue essay by Gerhard Finckh, Museum Folkwang, Essen
Angelika Storm-Rusche, *Neue Zeit*, Berlin, 2 April
'A sense of purpose', catalogue essay by Michael Tooby, Mappin Art Gallery, Sheffield
Sue Hubbard, *Time Out*, November

1993   'Yuko Shiraishi', catalogue essay by Mel Gooding, Gallery Kasahara, Osaka
'Moving into View - Recent British painting', catalogue essay by Sacha Craddock, Arts Council, London
'Zwei Energien', catalogue essay by Thomas A. Clark;

'Japan-Aspekte eines Landes und einer Gesellschaft' by Margit Weinberg-Staber, Haus für Konstruktive und Konkrete Kunst, Zurich
William Packer, *Financial Times*, 14 May
Nicoletta Locarnini, *Arte*, June
'Junge Kunst Sammeln 93', catalogue essay by Heinrich Klotz, Daimler Benz, Stuttgart

1994 Lucinda Bredin, *Sunday Telegraph*, 12 June
Geraldine Norman, *Independent on Sunday*, 31 July
Martin Gayford, *Sunday Telegraph*, 21 August
William Packer, *Financial Times*, 10 September
John McEwen, *Sunday Telegraph*, 18 September
John Windsor, *Independent on Sunday*, 18 September
William Packer, *Financial Times*, 24 September
Martin Gayford, *Modern Painters*, Autumn

1995 Sister Wendy Beckett, *Meditations of Silence*, published by Dorling Kindersley
Sarah Kent, *Time Out*, 22-9 November
Sue Hubbard, *New Statement and Society*, December

1996 Monograph *Yuko Shiraishi*, Cantz'sche Verlag, Germany: 'Harmony that puts order into contradiction' by Dr Volker Rattemeyer; 'Natural Selection' by Waldemar Januszczak; 'A Thin Irregular Yellow Line' by Thomas A. Clark; 'Torrential Rain' by Yuko Shiraishi
Sabine Weder Arlitt, 'Gedehnte Einsichten', *Tages-Anzeiger Zuritip*, Zurich, 31 May
Sibylle Omlin, *Neue Zürcher Zeitung*, 23 July
Heinz Norbert Jocks, *Westdeutsche Allgemeine Zeitung*, 24 October
Antje Klose, *Rheinische Post*, 26 October
Linda Rohr-Bongard, *Impulse*, November
'Focus', catalogue essay by Richard Grayson: '"Not quite" Some works by Yuko Shiraishi', 'Focus', catalogue essay by Yuko Shiraishi, Experimental Art Foundation, Australia

1997 Linda Maria Walker, *Broadsheet*, Vol.26 Autumn, Australia
'Pretext Heteronymous', catalogue essay by Achille Bonito Oliva, Juliet Steyn and Stella Santacatterina
'Juxtapositions', catalogue essay by Caoímhin Mac Giolla Leith, Annely Juda Fine Art, London
Michael Muridsany, *Le Figaro*, 1 October
Sacha Craddock, *The Times*, 18 November
Sue Hubbard, *Time Out*, 10-17 October

1998 'Abstraction and Melancholy', catalogue essay by Ildiko D. Udvary
'Yuko Shiraishi', catalogue essay by Norbert Lynton, Ernst Museum, Budapest, Hungary

'Clear and Saturated', catalogue essay by Yuko Shiraishi for Arti et Amicitiae, Amsterdam

1999 'As Dark as Light', catalogue interview with Michael Tooby, Tate St Ives, Cornwall
'Geometrie als Gestalt', catalogue essay by Fritz Jacobi, Neue Nationalgalerie, Berlin, Germany
Jonathan Jones, *The Guardian*, 1 June
Andrew Lambirth, *RA Magazine*, Summer
Charles Darwent, *The Sunday Independent*, 6 June
Camilla Blechen, *Frankfurter Allgemeine Zeitung*, 14 June
Ossian Ward, *The Art Newspaper*, July - August
Valerie Reardon, *Art Monthly*, July - August
Rachel Campbell-Johnston, *The Times*, 28 July
Sue Hubbard, *Contemporary Visual Arts*, Summer - Autumn
John McEwen, *The Sunday Telegraph*, 8 August
Ennio Puchard, *Lanedi*, 9 August
William Packer, *Financial Times*, 10 August
Katie Tokus, *Evening Herald*, 14 August
J. Koplos, *Art in America*, October

2000 Marion Benz, *Basler Zeitung*, 22-28 June

2001 'Assemble – Disperse', catalogue essay by Yuko Shiraishi; 'Globalisation, Identity, Culture, Art and A World of My Own', Annely Juda Fine Art, London

M. Wilsher, *What's On*, 20-30 May
M. Coomer, *Time Out*, 23 - 30 May
'Towards the forest of colour and regeneration', catalogue essay by Takeshi Sakurai, Gallery Kasahara, Tokyo

2002 Yuko Shiraishi, 'FIH - Field Institute Hombroich, Germany', *Landscape & Art*, Number 25
'Colour - A life of its own', catalogue essay by Livia Paldi, Mûcsarnok, Budapest
'Die unendliche Linie, The Infinite Line', catalogue essays by Volker Rattemeyer, Renate Petzinger, Katja Blomberg, Museum Wiesbaden
'Episode', catalogue essays by Sarah Shalgosky, Helen Legg and Nigel Walsh, 'Free Will' by Yuko Shiraishi, 'Whispered Asides: The paintings of Yuko Shiraishi' by Marco Livingstone, 'Painting and Photography' by Andrew Benjamin
Karen Write, *Modern Painters*, Winter 2002
Rose Aiden, *Vogue*, November

2003 Mark Ewart, *The Irish Times*, 28 April
Nicola Jackson, 'Building The BBC: A return to Form' BBC publications, London
'Tuesday is cerise', 'Making Space', catalogue essay by Richard Grayson

2004 'Was ist Kunst?' by Angela Thomas-Schmid, *Du* June

2005 Manfred Eichel, *Zeitraum*, 32
'Temperature' catalogue essay by Ian Hunt 'Latent Heat', Annely Juda Fine Art, London

ISBN 1-904621-06-6

Photographs:
Bob Barry, Tate Gallery, St Ives; Colin Davison, Waygood Gallery;
Nick Guttridge, BBC London; Jimbo, Insel Hombrich;
Ian Parker, London; Dara McGrath, Crawford Municipal Art Gallery, Cork;
Ed Restle, Museum Wiesbaden; John Riddy, London; József Rosta, Mûcsarnok, Budapest

Printed by BAS Printers Ltd, England

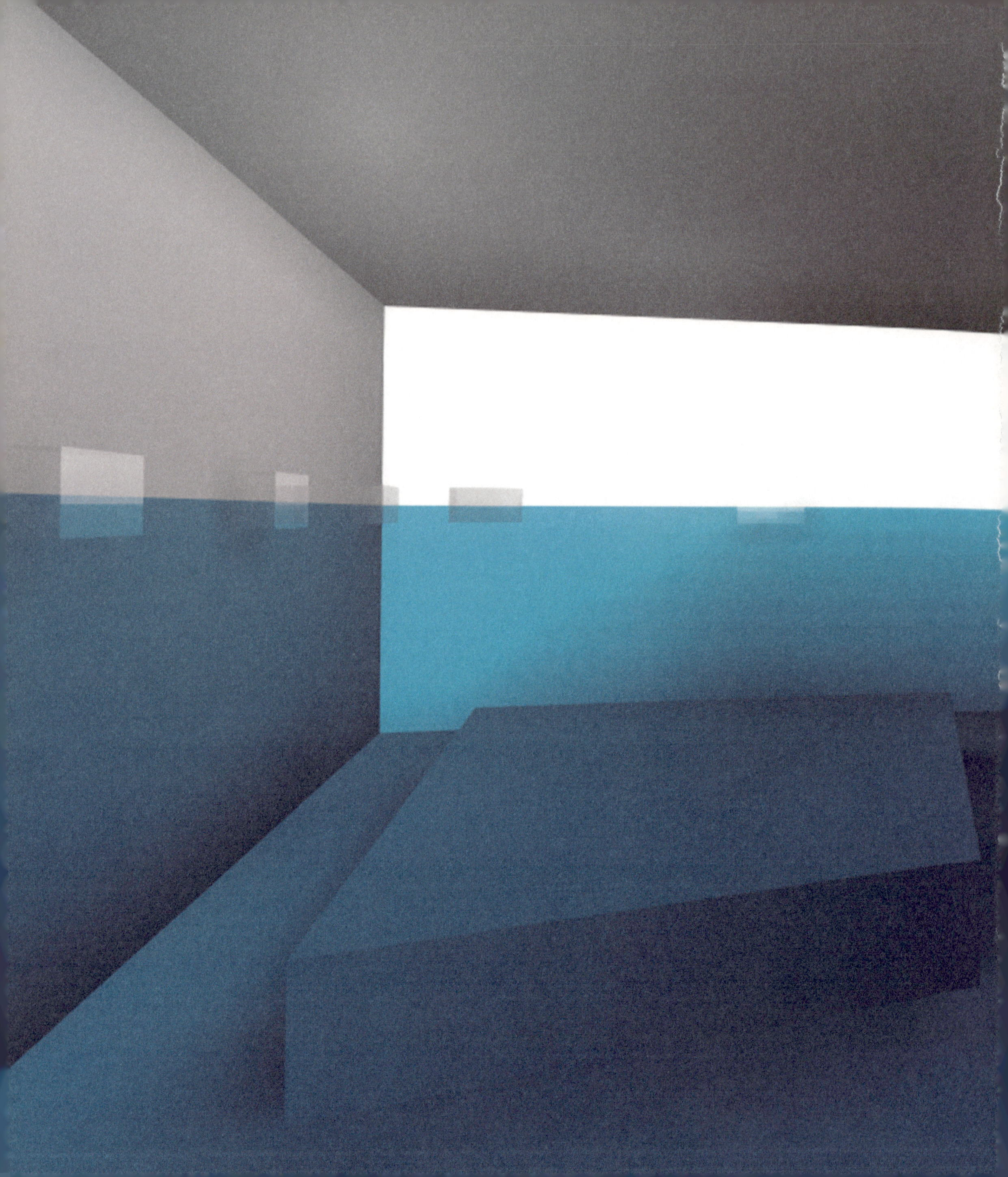